Blessings to
your dear friend!

FACELESS

UNRAVELING THE
MYSTERY OF IDENTITY

DIANE M. FINK

May you be encouraged
in the YOU God made
you to be!

Diane

Faceless: Unraveling the Mystery of Identity
ISBN: 978-1-6092014-5-6
Printed in the United States of America
©2021 by Diane M. Fink, All rights reserved.
Updated Edition-2008
Original printing 2002

Library of Congress Number: 2008935118
Unless otherwise noted, all Scripture quotations are from the Holy
Bible, New King James Version. Copyright© 1979, 1980, 1982,
Thomas Nelson, Inc. Other versions abbreviated as follows: NIV (New
International Version), TAB (The Amplified Bible), The Message, The
Jerusalem Bible.

Ajoyin Publishing, Inc.
P.O. 342
Three Rivers, MI 49093 www.ajoyin.com

Please direct your inquiries to admin@ajoyin.com

FACELESS

UNRAVELING THE MYSTERY OF IDENTITY

DIANE M. FINK

ENDORSEMENTS

Dr. Dan Hammer, Apostolic Leader

Diane Fink has written a great book – *Unraveling the Mystery of Identity.* This book deals with your unique identity and how God wants you to realize who He has made you to be. Come face-to-face with God and let Him show you where He will heal, strengthen, and identify you! You will no longer be "faceless." Diane's practical teaching will help you discover your true identity.

I highly recommend Diane as an author, speaker, and teacher. I have been her pastor for about 30 years and vouch for her godly character and giftedness.

Senior Apostolic Leader
Seattle Bible College President
SEND Network Founder
Sonrise Christian Center
Everett, Washington

Adam Narciso
Speaker & Author, *New Identity: 30 Days of Prayer for Spiritual Transformation*

I'm convinced that one of the most powerful functions of the prophetic is to restore one's identity. A word from the Father that highlights the unique design and dignity of one of his kids is a divine interruption. It disrupts the demonic narrative playing in people's minds about themselves. Such words carry the potential for healing and transformation.

What Diane Fink has produced is a resource that does exactly that. Laced with transparent insights from her own story, principles of transformation, and practical application prompts, *Faceless* is a powerful tool for anyone who yearns for a deeper answer to the age-old question everyone needs to answer: who am I?
Graham Cooke, Author, Speaker, Publisher:

Our true identity must impact our behavior because identity is the key to transformation. When we know who we are in Jesus, and more importantly, who He is for us, then we can learn how to stand and walk in the Holy Spirit. This book helps us to navigate our way into a present-future mindset and lifestyle. Diane takes us on a journey that enables us to understand the development process of growing up into all things in Christ.

Oregon:
I learned that knowing who I am is a much greater agent of change than doing the right thing, how freeing.

Connecticut:
Word pictures like, 'my life is a tapestry' have helped me see that God has already stamped His picture on the fabric of me. The underside may contain loose ends and knots, but the thread continues on-love. The richness of His love is what I've been searching for since childhood. As a leader, I feel I can lead from a more steady/secure place.

Seattle, WA:
Clearly the best book I've ever read on identity.

Australia:
Every lesson had valuable keys that have helped to unlock and reveal the true identity I have in Jesus Christ...This book is clear and concise about the truth, yet beautifully explained. In opening every area of my heart to Him, and receiving His love, there is no room for distorted perceptions of myself or looking outwards for deep needs to be met.

Washington State:
A supernatural, inner transformation has equipped me with a sense of stability, an inner knowing that I cannot be shaken or moved from fulfilling God's plans and purposes for my life. This book restored a sense of who I am as a person, personally and spiritually.

This book, originally published as *True Identity*, has been used in small groups inside and outside the church, in prisons, as Leadership Training material in the Unites States and in many countries. It has even been used as a group study in the bull riding arena.

TABLE OF CONTENTS

FOREWORD

Identity. That topic has been the focus of my life and ministry for the last 20 years. It was the identity message that helped me overcome a broken self-image that became shattered through pornography addiction, guilt, shame, and self-hatred. I finally got to the point where I actually believed this: "Therefore, if anyone is in Christ, the new creation has come: The old has gone, the new is here" (2 Corinthians 5:27, NIV).

I walked in so much freedom from my past and eventually I thought that maybe I kind of had this whole identity message down. Well, life pressures and trials come in unexpected ways, and I would need this message many times over during the course of my journey with God.

Somehow, along the way I thought that understanding my identity in Christ almost meant ignoring myself or my feelings. We are called to deny ourselves in the sense that we don't allow our self to rule but submit to Jesus. However, I have learned that self-awareness has actually become a place where God meets me and I experience His promises. God doesn't work on our false self or our ideal self, but He meets us where we are at with authenticity.

Diane Fink has done such an awesome job in her book, *Faceless: Unraveling the Mystery of Identity,* to help the reader see how much they are loved while confronting lies and hindrances to their true identity. Diane is authentic. She is a blessing to my church and so faithfully lives out these realities in our community. She is an excellent storyteller and teacher. This is not a book that is theory, but is full of Scripture and lived experience putting that truth into practice.

Faceless is an invitation to have God set you free and help you see your true identity, design, and purpose. If you come with an open heart to God as you read this and allow God to confront the areas of unbelief and pain in your heart, you will be transformed by His truth.

This is a core message that is needed over and over to get from our heads to our hearts. This is a message that will be tried by the fires of life but will also keep us through the fires of life. As you start this book, be prepared for heart surgery, encouragement, healing, and transformation. You are loved more than you could imagine by a God who is even better than you think. He loves you the way you are, but He refuses to leave you the same.

John Hammer
Senior Pastor
Sonrise Christian Center, Everett, WA

ACKNOWLEDGEMENTS

Were I to list all those who have significantly "sewn" into my life and the tapestry of my own identity, it would take another whole book. There are some, however, that I must acknowledge without whom this book would not have happened.

First and foremost, Jesus Christ. From the first day I met You, my life has never been the same. YOU truly are the foundation and beginning place of our identity.

Pastors Dick and Marilyn Williamson. For your wisdom, godly counsel, loving truth, and special friendship. Marilyn, I know you are enjoying the eternal fruit of all your labor while here on earth...and the countless lives you touched. We're grateful for the time we had you with us.

Jane Hansen Hoyt. Heart-to-heart friendships like ours don't come along often in a lifetime. I'm grateful for the love and joys, tears and sorrows, we've shared through the years...for each experience has only served to deepen the bond between us. Friend to confide in. Mentor to learn from...I have watched you lead with grace and wisdom and have gained much. You have enriched my life.

Pastor Dan Hammer. Pastor Herb Marks. Joan Bennett. Avril Vandermerwe. Bonnie Fretwell. Deena Wilson. Pam Eichorn at Ajoin Publishing. What strong and beautiful "threads" each of you has sewn into my life.

Karen E. Anderson. "Editor of the World" ...Editor Extraordinaire! Not only your expertise (of which there is much), but your friendship and love.

Jennie Newbrough. For encouraging and believing in who I am in Him. Friend. Colleague. Co-laborer in the Kingdom. Your input has been invaluable.

I could go on...so many are the gifted, talented, caring, encouraging, special people in my life, whom I value and cherish.

My family. Our four wonderful daughters, from whom I've learned more than I can say.
Our grandchildren...the delight and joy of my life.

My late husband, Chuck. Your steadfast, unconditional love always allowed me to be the person God created me to be. You have sewn into the fabric of my life more than you realized when you were here on earth.

I trust that, now in heaven, you know how much I loved you and how grateful I am for the way you loved me. I miss you greatly, but know you are enjoying your reward in Heaven. Till I see you again, my love…

INTRODUCTION

Walking down the produce aisle, I spotted her turning into my path and heading for the Honeycrisp apples I was loading into the plastic bag. I grabbed one more apple and plunked the bag into my cart and, averting my eyes from hers, dashed off to the cereal aisle. Who was she? Someone I'd known several years ago when we were in a study group together. Unsure that she would remember me, I sprinted off to get my Cheerios and finish shopping rather than risk saying hello.

Do you want to know why I didn't stop to say, "Hi! Remember me? We were in that study group together a few years ago"? I couldn't be sure she'd remember me, and I'd feel foolish if I greeted her and she didn't have a clue who I was.

The root of that behavior goes clear back to my childhood and the dysfunction, alcoholism, and domestic violence in our home. I didn't have much of a relationship with my father even though he was in the home until I was twelve years old. He was emotionally absent and unavailable. What little communication there was, usually contained demeaning sarcastic remarks.

Years later, through counseling, I came to realize the significant impact a father has on the identity of his daughter. Because I lacked a healthy relationship with my father, I grew up with a rather unusual concept of myself. In my mind's eye, my face was nothing more than a blank oval – no features, no distinguishing marks. Therefore, I would never approach someone, like the lady in the grocery store, unless I was sure the person knew me. Being "faceless" meant being unrecognizable.

Our face instantly distinguishes us one from another. It reveals the uniqueness of God's creation when He made each of us in His image. In a sense, it is representative of our personal identity. Life's trauma, pain, and brokenness, have a way of shaping our identity, distorting the image God had in mind when He created us. Even though life experiences have influenced us, they cannot define us, unless we let them.

This book is about the journey of rediscovering the unique individuality of your true identity. You are not like anyone else on the face of the earth and that is by design. God had an amazing YOU in mind when He knit you together in your mother's womb (Psalm 139:13) and saw to it that every stitch was woven with His love and purpose for your life. It's as if God is creating a beautiful tapestry of all our lives corporately, and of each of our lives individually. My prayer is that you will release any "stitches" the enemy and the world have woven into your life, and you will discover the wonderful identity and destiny God has in store for you.

Enjoy the journey!

THE TAPESTRY

Picture a tapestry…a heavy cloth, woven with decorative designs and pictures, often used as a wall hanging. It is usually a beautiful work of art which you might see hanging in a museum or an art gallery. Intricately designed, artfully and skillfully wrought, it is a highly valued work of embroidery or needlework.

Tapestries date as far back as 1500 BC and are evident in the cultural history of many ancient civilizations including Egypt, Peru, China, Greece, and throughout Europe. The process was quite involved and considerable time was needed to create a tapestry. It began with a painting or drawing on linen or paper, usually by a noted artist, which was then copied by the one weaving the tapestry. Only the best materials were used: fine wool, silk, linen, various kinds and colors of threads. Many of the older tapestries were even woven with gold thread.

A Process

God has been in the process of weaving a tapestry since He first spoke, "Let there be light." He has taken great care because His tapestry has divine purpose woven into each strand. Some stitches are worked in bold, vibrant colors with strong, thick yarn. Some are soft, muted shades. Some are pastels, light and fresh. Some of the needlework is fine, precisely sewn stitches using delicate threads.

Each one of us individually is a part of His tapestry. Corporately, He is weaving us together to create a self-portrait through which He can express Himself to His creation. That is His purpose in the earth: to have a people who will represent His image, His nature, His character, to those who are hurting, broken, lonely, and without hope. God's heart is always toward the yet-to-be-redeemed. As we allow His Spirit to do a work of restoration in our lives, we will be better able to express His heart to the world.

As we will see in a later chapter, God is also creating a unique tapestry of each of our personal lives according to the design He had in mind when

He created us. Ephesians 2:10 states that...*we are God's workmanship, created in Christ Jesus to do good works, which God prepared in advance for us to do* (NIV). It's as if He began with a clean piece of cloth and imprinted upon it His design (identity) for our lives and proceeded carefully and purposefully to stitch it with His loving hands.

Distortions

The problem is that others have "woven" things into our lives as well – knowingly or unknowingly – distorting and detracting from God's original design for us. Living from a distorted or damaged identity results in any number of issues ranging from unrealized potential to relational breakdown.

Because our identity directly affects the way we relate to the world in which we live, it is essential that we understand places in us where wounds and hurts have distorted our self-concept. We can be unaware of those areas. But, if we are open to God working in our hearts, He can show us, by the way we respond to life's situations, those places in us that need healing.

He wants to reveal to us HIS design, HIS plan, and HIS purpose for our lives so that we can be the distinctive individuals He created us to be. It has been said that the greatest gift someone can give you is their difference from you. God is a God of diversity... He who made each snowflake different, fashioned you specially and unlike anyone else. Think of how boring a tapestry would be if it had all the same colors, the same kind of thread, and uniform stitches!

Identity is a foundational issue. It is why God has been highlighting it in His body. So much of our life and relationships flow out of who we believe we are, what we perceive our value to be, and where we see our life going. You may not give it much thought in the course of your day-to-day life as you go to the office or factory or job site, make doctor appointments, grocery shop, run errands, mow the grass, or shuttle kids to soccer practice. But identity is a subject that affects every aspect of your life. Your identity, or the way you perceive yourself in the context of your world, colors the hopes, dreams, goals, and desires for your life. Your identity affects your relationships, positively or negatively, with God, spouse, children, relatives, friends, and co-workers.

A Healthy Self-Concept

Let me give you a simple illustration. If, as a child, you grew up with loving affirmation from your parents, your relationship with God (your heavenly Father) is more likely to be healthier than someone who did not receive that from their family of origin. It's probable that trusting God would come easier for you than for someone who did not receive the security of a parent's love and acceptance. You might be willing to risk pursuing a career or ministry goal that may seem beyond your reach if you are confident in who you are as a person. Even your relationships with others would tend to be stronger because you would be relating from a place of proper self-perception rather than feeling threatened by relationship.

When I attended a secular seminar on the topic of conflict resolution, I found it interesting that the first and most important block to resolving conflict satisfactorily was identified as a healthy self-concept. You see, most of us relate to others based on who we believe we are, who we think we should be, or what we think others expect us to be. Relating from a damaged or poor self-concept can result in relational dysfunction and conflict.

As we will see in a later chapter, while it may not be parents alone who help to "weave" a person's identity, family does play a significant role. That was God's purpose in establishing families: to provide a safe environment in which a child could develop physically, emotionally, and spiritually into the person God designed, thus fulfilling His purpose for his or her life. Unfortunately, those whom God intended to be the teachers, trainers, and nurturers (Deuteronomy 6:7, Proverbs 22:6, Ephesians 6:4), that is, parents, all too often have themselves grown up with an unclear or distorted identity resulting from the dysfunction in their families of origin. But God is greater! He is able to restore all that the enemy has taken (Joel 2:25-27).

Knitted In Love

A wonderful story by Max Lucado poignantly touches this issue of identity within each one of us that is at once so basic and yet so profound. It resonates deep within and speaks to the very core of our being.

In my closet hangs a sweater that I seldom wear. It is too small. The sleeves are too short, the shoulders too tight. Some of the buttons are missing, and the thread is frazzled. I should throw that sweater away. I have no use for it. I'll never wear it again. Logic says I should clear out the space and get rid of the sweater. That's what logic says. But love won't let me. Something unique about that sweater makes me keep it.

What is unusual about it? For one thing, it has no label.

Nowhere on the garment will you find a tag that reads, 'Made in Taiwan,' or 'Wash in cold water.' It has no tag because it wasn't made in a factory. It has no label because it wasn't produced on an assembly line. It isn't the product of a nameless employee earning a living. It's the creation of a devoted mother expressing her love.

That sweater is unique. One of a kind. It can't be replaced. Each strand was chosen with care. Each thread was selected with affection. And though the sweater has lost all of its use, it has lost none of its value. It is valuable not because of its function, but because of its maker. That must have been what the psalmist had in mind when he wrote, 'You knit me together in my mother's womb.' [1]

Can you relate? Have you ever felt like you've been hanging in a dark closet for longer than you care to remember? Have you ever felt ill-fitted to the world in which you live, worn out, or worse, like damaged goods? Have you ever questioned why you are even on this blue orb we call Earth and if there is a purpose in this reality we call life? If so, you have grappled with an area that is the very foundation of who you are: your identity.

ORIGINAL DESIGN
Identity Defined

What do we mean by "identity?" Simply put, it is the way we see ourselves. It is a set of beliefs, conscious or unconscious, we hold to be true about who we are. It is, in a sense, the very fabric of our being.

Webster's Dictionary defines identity as, *the condition or fact of being a specific person or thing; individuality.* The word also has the meaning of being the same as. We refer to twins that are of the same sex and look very much alike as "identical" twins.

We are all familiar with the term "identity theft." It's become a multimillion-dollar crime industry based on stealing people's identities and personal information. Phishing, smishing, robo-phone calls-it always appears to come from a trusted source, when it is from an imposter. Spiritually, we face an enemy "imposter"who wants to steal not only our resources, but our God-given identity as image-bearers on the earth.

Another term you are probably familiar with is "identity crisis." Often occurring in adolescents, it's a feeling of uncertainty about who they are and where they are going in life. Their uncertainty stems from the fact that they are in transition to adulthood: no longer children, not yet fully adults.

An identity crisis can occur in a woman when her children are grown and leave the home. Some call it "empty nest syndrome." Her role as mother seemingly has ended abruptly, leaving her to wonder how to relate to her world when everything has changed. Retirement, especially for men, can trigger a loss of identity. The job that defined their lives for many years is no longer there. Husbands or wives can experience an identity crisis when they lose a spouse, particularly after many years of marriage. Widowhood is an entirely unknown identity to the newly bereaved, one that is difficult to embrace.

While we may go through times when our identity is seemingly shaken or transformed by outward circumstances, the core of who we are, our DNA does not change. Unfortunately, we don't always know our true identity in the depth of our being. The world and the enemy have so distorted our perception of ourselves that we function out of false beliefs instead of the truth.

Two Elements of Identity

Two components that make up our identity are SECURITY and SIGNIFICANCE. Security has to do with our sense of who we are as individuals stemming from a feeling of acceptance and perceived value or worth.

Security

To feel secure and worthwhile, we must know that we are loved with the kind of love that we cannot earn, and therefore, cannot lose based on our actions. We are secure when someone knows our weaknesses, failures, and sin, but loves us still. It's a place of safety where we can be real and know that we will be accepted and valued.

It has been said that the greatest single cause of a poor self-concept is the absence of unconditional love. I know of only three persons who can love that way: the Father, the Son, and the Holy Spirit. God's love for you is such that there is nothing you can do to make Him love you more than He does right this moment. Nor is there anything that can make Him love you less. He loves you without condition.

Significance

Significance is the need to know that your life has meaning, that there is purpose in your existence. Another word for it is destiny. Deep within is a desire to know that your life can have impact, that there is a reason you are here, and that you are adequate to fulfill your purpose. Knowing that you are part of something larger than yourself gives you a sense of purpose and value.

As we will see, an identity that is not founded in God will lead to pursuing significance through what the world has to offer: a prestigious job (or ministry), financial success, fame, power, etc. The list goes on and on. But once again, there is only one source of true significance – God. As our Creator, He knows the plans and purposes He has for us, and they are good (Jeremiah 29:11).

A healthy self-concept, or identity, grows from knowing we are loved and accepted, that we have value, and that our life has meaning and purpose.

Who You Are In Christ

As a believer, your true identity can be expressed through the following verses:

Genesis 1:26
Then God said, "Let Us make man in Our image, according to Our likeness; let them have dominion over the fish of the sea, over the birds of the air, and over the cattle, over all the earth and over every creeping thing that creeps on the earth."

We were HIS idea — made in the image of God Almighty, the Creator of all things!

2 Corinthians 5:17
Therefore, if anyone is in Christ, he is a new creation; old things have passed away; behold, all things have become new.

We get a brand-new start when we come to Jesus – the slate is wiped clean!

Ephesians 1:6
…to the praise of the glory of His grace, by which He has made us accepted in the Beloved.

We are accepted by Him, therefore we are acceptable!

2 Corinthians 5:21
For He made Him who knew no sin to be sin for us, that we might become the righteousness of God in Him.

Jesus became who we were so that we could become who He is – the righteousness of God!

John 1:12-13
But as many as received Him, to them He gave the right to become children of God, to those who believe in His name: who were born, not of blood, nor of the will of the flesh, nor of the will of man, but of God.

Children of God – born into His wonderful family!

Romans 8:14-17
For as many as are led by the Spirit of God, these are sons of God.
For you did not receive the spirit of bondage again to fear, but you received the Spirit of adoption by whom we cry out, "Abba, Father."
The Spirit Himself bears witness with our spirit that we are children of God, and if children, then heirs—heirs of God and joint heirs with Christ, if indeed we suffer with Him, that we may also be glorified together.

Our earthly heritage exchanged for His heavenly heritage!

Familiar scriptures, aren't they? And most of us who are believers would say we know that these verses are true. Yet, as we go through this book, we'll see that what we believe with our minds may not be a true reflection of our heart beliefs which are evidenced through our behavior, emotions, and attitudes.

"Head Knowledge" vs. "Heart Knowledge"

We often give mental assent and are in total agreement with what the Word of God states. However, when it comes to walking it out, the truth we hold in our heart will be expressed through our actions. It is the difference between "head knowledge" and "heart knowledge." Head knowledge gives assent to, agrees with, and even desires to live according to the truth of the Word. Heart knowledge, or the deep beliefs we hold to be true, is expressed through our words, actions, emotions, and attitudes (Luke 6:45).

The "heart" represents our inner being and is the fountain of all we do (Proverbs 4:23). An example of the difference between head and heart knowledge would be someone who says the words of the sinner's prayer to receive salvation, without any change in their life. That's "mental assent" to the need for salvation. However, someone who has seen their need for Jesus deep within, not only says the words, but prays from the heart, resulting in a change in their life (Romans 10:9-10). That is heart knowledge.

In John 8:32, Jesus states: *And you shall know the truth and the truth shall make you free.* The word translated "know" is the Greek word *ginosko* and it means "the recognition of truth by personal experience."[2] That is much more than just knowing something as a fact; it is heart knowledge. In the case of salvation, it is a personal encounter with the Truth that goes beyond mental understanding to the very depth of the heart. To put it another way: *Such "knowledge" is obtained, not by mere intellectual activity, but by operation of the Holy Spirit consequent upon acceptance of Christ.*[3]

When we enter a relationship with Jesus Christ through salvation, we open our heart to Him and the Holy Spirit who is then able to bring recognition, understanding, and acceptance of the truth of the Word of God. What is the truth we need to know by experience? It is God's love for us, acceptance of us, and the value He sees in us. We need to know that He has a planned purpose and destiny for our lives.

As He Thinketh...

Why is heart knowledge so important to the topic of identity? Because we are told in Proverbs 23:7, *For as he thinks in his heart, so is he.* Who we are and what we become has much to do with the way we think about ourselves in our heart.

The word translated, *thinks*, means "to split open, reason out, reckon, estimate."[4] It actually comes from a word for "an opening, a door or gate."[5] We already defined heart as the inner being. One final significant word in this verse is the word "so." It means to establish or fix. Putting these definitions together, we understand the verse to say:

AS A PERSON REASONS, RECKONS, OR ESTIMATES HIMSELF TO BE IN HIS INNER BEING, SO IT IS ESTABLISHED AND FIXED: THAT IS WHO HE IS!

Closed Door

If you are only open to seeing yourself in one way, the door is closed to perceiving yourself in any other light or truth. If, due to wounding, trauma, neglect, or other damaging experiences, you have perceived yourself as unworthy or inadequate, that is how you define yourself as a person.

Woven into the fabric of your being are heart beliefs and perceptions so deep, that even the Word of God cannot be fully embraced. You heard the lie before you heard the truth, now you hear the truth of God through the lie. But God is able! As you choose to open those places in your heart to Him, He will impart to you HIS identity, HIS destiny, HIS plan and purpose for your life.

Let's Talk About It

1. Share with the group how you would describe your identity. Have experiences from the past affected the way you perceive yourself? Share one or two examples.
2. What are your heart feelings as you read the verses related to who you are in Christ? Do you think it is more of a mental assent or "heart knowledge" for you at this point in your life?
3. When have you seen behaviors, emotions, or attitudes that betray what you truly believe about yourself?
4. Have you personally experienced the truth that you are a child of God? A joint heir with Jesus? The righteousness of God? Share what that means to you.
5. Do you know "by experience" the kind of love that you cannot earn and therefore, you cannot lose, based on your behavior?

At Home This Week

Meditate on the scriptures in this chapter, looking them up in various translations of the Bible to gain fresh perspective on them. Write out in your own words what they mean to you.

Truth to Embrace

1. Two components that make up our identity are security and significance. Security has to do with our sense of who we are as individuals stemming from a feeling of acceptance and perceived value or worth.
2. Significance is the need to know that your life has meaning, that there is purpose in your existence. Another word for it is destiny.
3. As a person reasons, reckons, or estimates himself to be in his inner being, so it is established and fixed: that is who he is!

WHAT'S IN A NAME?

That which we call a rose by any other name would smell as sweet.
— William Shakespeare

Shakespeare was right. Were we to identify a rose by another name, say daisy or daffodil, it would change neither the beauty nor the sweet fragrance of the flower. It would not change its essence, or identity. We have come to know this family of plants as roses and can identify them easily by some of their characteristics – color, shape, and fragrance. When someone says the word "rose," you know exactly what she is referring to. Names are significant and are very closely associated with identity.

Biblical Names

Names were of great significance in biblical times and were given for several different reasons. Sometimes, a child was named because of a certain characteristic. Esau's name means "hairy" which reflected his appearance (Genesis 25:25).

Some names were given to signify a national event in the history of the nation of Israel, as in 1 Samuel 4:19-22. A baby born to Phinehas' wife was named, Ichabod. The Philistines had captured the Ark of the Covenant and her husband and father-in-law (Eli) had died. To commemorate the darkness of the time, she named her son Ichabod, which means *the glory has departed from Israel.*

Names were given to reflect the circumstances of the child's birth or the parent's feeling at the time. Moses was so named because he was *drawn out of the water.* Isaac means *laughter* and expressed his mother's joy at his birth.

Character or Nature

People in the Bible believed there was a vital connection between a person and their name. The meaning of names was important because it signified character, nature, and destiny.

Nowhere is this principle more clearly illustrated than in the names of God. Throughout Scripture, God unfolded His nature to His people through word pictures. He was weaving a self-portrait, expressing His identity through His names and His encounters with Israel.

At the burning bush, God revealed Himself to Moses as I AM WHO I AM (Exodus 3:14)...eternal, self-existent one.

In Exodus 6:3-4, Moses receives a new revelation of God: I *appeared to Abraham, to Isaac, and to Jacob, as God Almighty, but by My name, LORD, I was not known to them.*

LORD, or Jehovah, is the personal name of God as opposed to God Almighty (El Shaddai), which means the all-powerful, self-sufficient God.

Jehovah – A New Revelation

This new revelation as "Jehovah" expressed the covenantal relationship of God to His people. It also signified that the way was now open for the Israelites to know God personally.

We read in Exodus 34:5-7, that the Lord proclaimed His name to Moses by describing His character and attributes: ...*merciful and gracious, long-suffering, and abounding in goodness and truth, keeping mercy for thousands, forgiving iniquity and transgression and sin, by no means clearing the guilty...*

God continues to develop the tapestry of His nature and character throughout the Word by means of His names.

The Names of God

Jehovah Tsidkenu
    The Lord our Righteousness   (Jeremiah23:6, 33:16)
Jehovah M'Kaddesh
    The Lord our Sanctifier   (Exodus 31:13)
Jehovah Shalom
    The Lord our Peace   (Judges 6:24)
Jehovah Shammah
    The Lord our Ever-Present One   (Ezekiel 48:35)
Jehovah Rapha
    The Lord our Healer   (Exodus 15:26)

Jehovah Jireh
> The Lord our Provider   (Genesis 22:14)

Jehovah Nissi
> The Lord our Banner   (Exodus 17:15)

Jehovah Rohi
> The Lord our Shepherd   (Psalm 23:1)

There are other word pictures of God's nature as well, but He is seen in His fullness in the person of His Son, Jesus.

He is the sole expression of the glory of God – the Light-being, the out-raying of the divine – and He is the perfect imprint and very image of [God's] nature…(Hebrews 1:3, AMP).

For in Him dwells all the fullness of the Godhead bodily (Colossians 2:9).

Jesus said, *He who has seen Me has seen the Father* (John 14:9).

Jesus also states that He has manifested the name of the Father (John 17:6), meaning He has revealed the divine nature of God to men. Jesus' own character was described through Isaiah's prophecy:

And His name will be called, Wonderful, Counselor, Mighty God, Everlasting Father, Prince of Peace (Isaiah 9:6).

Authority

Names also denote authority and power. In the New Testament, Jesus instructs that whatever we ask in His name, He will do, that the Father may be glorified in the Son. *If you ask anything in My name, I will do it* (John 14:13-14).

Mark 16:17-18: *In My name they will cast out demons; they will speak with new tongues; they will take up serpents; and if they drink anything deadly, it will by no means hurt them; they will lay hands on the sick, and they will recover.*

The disciples healed in the authority and power of the name of Jesus (Acts 3:6-7, Acts 4:7-10).

You can see this principle of names representing authority in operation even in the modern workplace. If you were asked by the CEO of the company to do a project, how much more quickly would you get it done than if the receptionist asked you to do it!

Destiny

In the Bible, names were also given to signify destiny, or purpose. Noah, whose name means, "rest," was destined to bring rest, and comfort, to his family when God's judgment came on the earth in the form of the flood (Genesis 5:29).

Elijah ministered at a time in Israel's history when the king and queen had established the worship of Baal in the land. Elijah's name means, "Jehovah is God." Every time Elijah's name was spoken, it was a declaration of the truth that Jehovah is God in Israel, not Baal!

Jesus' name, too, bespeaks His destiny:

And she will bring forth a Son, and you shall call His name JESUS, for He will save His people from their sins (Matthew 1:21).

So we see that names have significance in the Bible for several reasons: identifying characteristics, remembering a national event, reflecting the circumstances of birth, or the parent's feelings at the time. The most meaningful aspect of a name is that it is linked to the very identity of a person: character, nature, and destiny.

Let's Talk About It

1. How have you experienced any of the aspects of God's character represented by His names as listed in this chapter? Are there other names of God you have personally experienced?
2. God is first, "Father." Is it easy for you to relate to God as your Father? If so, why? If not, why do you think that is?
3. Can you share about a time when you called on the authority in the name of Jesus? What was the result?

At Home This Week

Look up some of the names God calls us. (His children, joint heirs with Christ, the Bride of Christ, etc.) Then ask God to anchor them in your heart.

Truth to Embrace

1. People in the Bible believed there was a vital connection between the name and the person it identified.
2. Names have significance in the Bible for several reasons. The names of God reflect His nature and character, His authority and power. Names given to individuals signify a person's purpose or destiny.
3. God continues to develop the tapestry of His nature and character throughout the Word by means of His names.

A NEW NAME

A Personal Journey

Several years ago, I was seeking the Lord for greater depth and intimacy in my relationship with Him. God takes us through seasons in our walk with Him when He stirs our hearts with a dissatisfaction and longing for more of Him. There was a hunger in my spirit to know Him more, a crying out for an increase of His presence in my life. So strong was the longing that I lived out of scriptures like Psalm 42:1-2:

> *As the deer pants for the water brooks,*
> *So pants my soul for You, O God. My soul thirsts for God,*
> *For the living God.*

Psalm 63:1 (AMP)
> *O God, You are my God; earnestly will I seek You; my inner self thirsts for You, my flesh longs and is faint for You, in a dry and weary land, where no water is.*

Psalm 84:2:
> *My soul longs, yes, even faints for the courts of the Lord; My heart and flesh cry out for the living God.*

I wanted God to reveal to me His ways, as He did to Moses, not just His acts as He did the Israelites (Psalm 103:7). So, I began crying out, seeking His face in the secret place where it was just the two of us.

One of the things I learned was this: When you seek God's face, He'll show you yours! I began to realize that, what began as seeking more intimacy with Him, became an identity journey. He began to reveal sources I thought would define my identity, especially people who were authority figures. It was a painful time. I thought I had dealt with many of these issues through counseling years before. I had received much healing, but God had more to do.

In the process of being fashioned into His tapestry, He continually works to cut away and unravel the unlovely stitches that have been sewn into our lives by the enemy, so that He can weave His character and likeness into us. Ultimately, the Lord led me to change my name from a nickname I had used most of my life, to my given name. It was important for me to leave behind the woundedness of the past and embrace my true identity in Christ...the identity He had given me from the beginning.

A Future Hope

A portion of Scripture that came alive to me during this time was Isaiah 62:1-5, 12. The Lord brought revelation on the issue of identity through this passage. Biblical prophecy declares future things in the plan and purposes of God, as here in Isaiah. In effect, it looks ahead to the completed tapestry even though it is still very much a "work in progress." Let's begin with the first three verses of Isaiah 62.

For Zion's sake I will not hold My peace,
And for Jerusalem's sake I will not rest,
Until her righteousness goes forth as brightness,
And her salvation as a lamp that burns.
The Gentiles shall see your righteousness, And all kings your glory.
You shall be called by a new name, *[emphasis added]*
Which the mouth of the LORD will name.
You shall also be a crown of glory
In the hand of the LORD,
And a royal diadem
In the hand of your God.

In this portion of Scripture, Isaiah, through the power of the Holy Spirit, foresees Jerusalem's future identity. Both Israel and Judah had experienced a long period of prosperity and power. Idolatrous pagan worship had become common place in Israel. While Judah had maintained an outward conformity to God's law, inwardly they were falling into moral and spiritual decline.

Much of the book of Isaiah speaks of God's imminent judgment upon the nation for having violated His holy covenant. The prophet could foresee the coming captivity, first of Israel, then Judah. Along with the warning, which was intended to turn them back to obedience to God, Isaiah also lays a foundation of hope and a promise for Israel's future redemption. The opening verses of chapter 62 speak to that hope and promise of restoration.

Destiny for Jerusalem

God declares that Israel's righteousness and salvation will be made evident to both Gentiles and all kings. He is saying that the true identity and destiny He intended for Jerusalem will come forth.

While the prophetic significance for the nation of Israel as God's chosen people is obvious in this passage, we can make application to the church as spiritual Jerusalem. This portion of Scripture has much to speak to us concerning our identity, personally and corporately. God will bring forth the church's true identity, just as He will in the nation of Israel. Other nations will see it and know that He is God!

A New Name

Verse two declares the Lord will give Jerusalem a new name: one that will express who she truly is.

God often changed people's names in the Bible.
- Abram became Abraham (Gen 17:1-8, Neh 9:7). Abram means, "exalted father" while Abraham means, "father of a multitude." In changing Abram's name, God was calling forth the greater destiny he had been created for. By adding an "h" to Abram - one of the letters of YaWHeH - it was as though God was imparting to him a portion of His own name[6], hence, a part of His nature.
- God changed Sarai's name to Sarah, including an "h" in her name as well. Sarai, "Princess," became Sarah, "The Princess," or "Queen," linking her in co-rulership with her husband and including her in the covenant promises (Gen 17:15-16). Both were being called out of the identity of their past, into a new land with a new identity and destiny in God.
- Jacob means "deceiver," a picture of his character before he wrestled with God. His name became Israel, "prince," after he struggled and succeeded in receiving God's blessing (Gen 32:27-28; 35:9-15). He was destined to become the head of the twelve tribes of Israel.
- Did you know Moses changed Joshua's name (Numbers 13:16)? It was Hoshea, which means "salvation." Moses changed it to Joshua, "Jehovah is salvation," knowing it would be through Jehovah that the Israelites would conquer Canaan.
- Daniel and his three friends (Hananiah, Mishael, and Azariah) had their names changed to Belteshazzar, Shadrach, Meshach, and Abed-Nego by King Nebuchadnezzar's chief eunuch (Dan 1:6-7). Their renaming was an attempt to destroy their identity

as Hebrews, establish them as Chaldeans, and turn them away from the God of their fathers. Each of their Hebrew names had something of God in them:

Daniel – *God is my Judge*
Hananiah – *The grace of the Lord*
Mishael – *He that is the strong God*
Azariah – *The Lord is a help*

The Chaldean names all had references to the idols worshipped in Babylon:

Belteshazzar – *Keeper of the hidden treasures of Bel*
Shadrach – *Inspiration of the sun* (which the Chaldeans worshipped)
Meshach – *Of the goddess Shach*
Abed-Nego – *Servant of the shining fire* (also worshipped)

The attempt of the Chaldeans to turn them from their true identity was unsuccessful, but the changing of their names was intended to move them away from their Hebrew heritage and religion and towards their "new" identity. Not incidentally, their new identity was as slaves!

This same practice is occurring in our world today. There are reports from an African nation detailing the abduction of young males for use as slaves by Islamic fundamentalists. To undermine and eradicate their heritage and identity, they are given Islamic names.

- Esther's Hebrew name was Hadassah, meaning myrtle (Esther 2:7). Myrtle trees have fragrant leaves and starry white blossoms and held spiritual significance for the Israelites as symbols of peace and joy (Zechariah 1:8-11). Esther became a source of peace and joy to her people when, in risking her own life, she saved them from utter destruction. Interestingly, Esther, her new name, means, "star."
- Jesus changed Simon's name to Peter following his declaration of Jesus as Messiah and Son of the living God (Matthew 16:18). Impulsive, impetuous, unstable Simon is called, Peter, the rock. Can't you just see Jesus smiling as He changes his name, calling forth Peter's true identity and destiny as one of the building stones in the early church? Jesus saw the potential in his disciple and called it forth prophetically through his name.
- Then there is Saul, who became Paul (Acts 13:9). Fitting that the disciple to the Gentiles should be given a Roman name!

In all of the instances above, a new name speaks of new character, new dignity, new favor, and new destiny. When God changes a name, it is often to impart a new identity for that which He is about to do in and through the person.

Let's Talk About It

1. What names do you call yourself? (Positive or negative.)
2. What names have you been called that have either been a source of pain or a source of encouragement?
3. Have you or someone you know changed his/her name? What was the significance of it?

At Home This Week

Read the accounts in this chapter of people whose names were changed. Note any insights the Holy Spirit gives you in relation to their character and/or nature before and after the change.

Truth to Embrace

1. An "h" was added to Abram and Sarai: Abraham and Sarah. By adding an "h" to their names, it was as though God was imparting a portion of His own name, hence, a part of His nature.
2. The process of being fashioned into God's tapestry means that He continually works to cut away and unravel the unlovely stitches that have been sewn into our lives by the enemy, so that He can weave His character and likeness in us.

TANGLED THREADS

Have you ever been to an amusement park "fun house"?
One of the things I liked to do as a child was to stand in front of all the strange mirrors that would change your shape in the funniest ways. One mirror would make you look very long and skinny. Another would make you look short and fat. Still another would make your body look like it had waves and curves where you knew there weren't any! The experiences we have in life can do to our self-perception what the mirrors in the fun house do to our reflection – distort and twist the way we see ourselves.

As we continue our study of Isaiah 62, we see that Isaiah was describing the distorted identity of Jerusalem which was a result of turning away from God. The first part of verse four states:

You shall no longer be termed Forsaken,
Nor shall your land any more
Be termed Desolate.

Forsaken and desolate. Accurate words to describe her condition during the captivity to Babylon. What comes to mind when you picture Jerusalem during the siege and subsequent captivity? I think of pictures I have seen from World War II: bombed out cities, nothing left for miles around except piles of bricks and rubble; homes and buildings reduced to smoking heaps, remnants of what once was. Empty streets and empty homes, everyone taken away captive.

Perhaps some of you reading this have not only seen pictures, but have lived through the pain and devastation of World War II, or other wars such as the Korean War, the Vietnam War, or the Gulf War. The world continues to live through the war on terrorism in the wake of the attacks on New York City and the Pentagon on September 11, 2001. Through television, and the internet, the images of war have been vividly imprinted on our minds. The words "forsaken" and "desolate" are well chosen.

In some ways, I believe the church today is in captivity...to the world and its system. A report released by Christian market researcher George Barna noted some discouraging results concerning the church in the United States:

- Only 15% of those who regularly attend a Christian church ranked their relationship with God as the top priority in their life.
- Three out of every four teenagers have engaged in at least one type of psychic or witchcraft-related activity (Ouija board, books, playing sorcery/witchcraft games, palm reading). Fewer than three of every 10 churched teenagers have received teaching from their church concerning the supernatural.
- A comparison of people's faith before and after 9/11 showed that five years after the attack, there was little change in faith-related areas such as religious behaviors, beliefs, spiritual commitment, and self-identity.[7]

According to Barna's research, American Christians are not as dedicated to their faith as they like to believe. While they feel faith is important, "their faith is rarely the focal point of their life or a critical factor in their decision-making."[8]

I share these statistics only to point out that the enemy of our souls would like nothing better than to hold the church captive to the world system he has deceptively set in place.

Forsaken and Desolate

In Hebrew, the word translated "forsaken," pictures a divorced or widowed woman of that culture and time. It speaks of a sense of bereavement, of being discarded, deserted, rejected, and alone. Isaiah 54:6: *For the Lord has called you like a woman forsaken and grieved in spirit, like a youthful wife when you were refused.*

Women who were divorced or widowed had no means of support and were often destitute. Forced to exist under a shroud of shame, they lived without love, without a sense of value, and without hope. "Desolate" is an equally harsh word. It speaks of devastation, barrenness, no life, and no future, a wasteland.

Both terms are names of reproach and shame. As I read about the condition of Jerusalem during the captivity, I couldn't help but think: "Hasn't this been the identity of countless believers in the church?" So many have lived their lives from a place of reproach and shame. Held captive to a past marked by rejection and abandonment, an orphan spirit becomes their identity.

Reproach is the opposite of favor. It means to find fault with, blame, criticize, disapprove of, or discredit. It speaks of condemnation and judgmentalism, of living with regret and shame over the failures and mistakes of the past.

I believe one of the most effective tools the enemy uses to keep us ineffective for God is condemnation. If he can keep you bound by an identity that has been distorted by brokenness, rejection, abandonment, trauma, or loss, he can hinder you from coming into the fullness of the identity God had in mind when He imprinted His design on the tapestry of your life.

If the enemy can blind you to your true identity, he can keep you from fully inheriting the destiny God has for you. The place God has purposed just for you in His ongoing plan in the earth will be left vacant.

Tangled Threads

The fabric of my identity was woven from a background of dysfunction, alcoholism, and domestic violence. All I could see was the underside of my tapestry with tangled threads, frayed ends, and stitches that seemed to go nowhere. I grew up without a sense of security because of the conflict in my parents' marriage. My father was physically in the home until I was twelve years old when they divorced, but he was not present emotionally or spiritually. It wasn't until years later that I realized how that affected my identity.

I learned that a father's influence impacts his daughter's identity as a woman. Because I lacked a healthy relationship with my father, I grew up with a rather unusual concept of myself. Whenever I pictured how I looked, my face was a blank oval with no distinguishing features. I felt I was unrecognizable. FACELESS! Because of that, I would never approach someone I knew unless I was sure he knew who I was. It was too risky…being "faceless" meant others wouldn't recognize me and then I would feel foolish.

Remember the difference between head and heart knowledge? I knew intellectually my face had distinctive features, but my behavior of not speaking to someone reflected the belief in my heart. This was not a conscious awareness. I simply acted out of what was in my heart. My distorted self-concept of being less than and of little value, was one I carried with me into adulthood. But as I will share in a later chapter, God is able to heal the most broken of His children and fully unravel all the tangled threads.

The Lie

The enemy weaves his intentions into our lives as well: his lie. I mentioned in the first chapter that most of us heard the lie before we heard the truth, so that now we hear the truth of God through the lie. That means we filter the truth of the Bible through a belief system that has been affected by the lie of the enemy. He uses the lie to keep you from discovering and embracing all God created you to be.

God has a purpose for your life, but so does Satan. His purpose is to distort, diminish, or destroy the image of God in you. If he can succeed, you will be one less person reflecting the light of Christ in the earth. Satan's strategy is to hinder God's plan from going forth in the earth and to keep the light of the Gospel hidden.

What is the lie? It is a belief system that says:
1. You are not enough.
2. God is not enough to make you enough.
3. You need something from the world to make you enough.[9]

It began back in the Garden. When Eve was tempted to eat of the Tree of the Knowledge of Good and Evil, Satan implied: "You are not enough the way you are. There is something lacking in you, you are not adequate or sufficient." The enemy also insinuated that God was not able to make her enough. The conclusion? She needed something from the world (the fruit) to make her sufficient. We have been believing the lie ever since.

The basis of the lie and its insidious intent is to cause us to live out of an identity of shame. Shame says there is something inherently wrong with me; I am flawed, damaged goods. The feeling attached to shame is that of being unlovable and worthless. It is different from guilt in that guilt focuses on the action (I made a mistake). Shame focuses on the person (I am a mistake).

Mephibosheth

There was a young man in the Bible who was well acquainted with shame. His name was Mephibosheth. His story is rich with insight for us today. When he was 5 years old, his grandfather, King Saul, and his father, Jonathan, were killed. The Word tells us that his nurse picked him up and they fled. But as she hurried to leave, she dropped him, and Mephibosheth fell and became lame in both feet (2 Samuel 4:4, NCV).

Interesting that it was a nurse who dropped him – one who cares for the sick, brings comfort, healing, and a safe environment. God had created a safe environment, the Garden, for the highest of His creation. But just as Mephibosheth "fell" from his nurse, so man "fell" and has been "lame" ever since. Mephibosheth was five years old when he fell. Five is the number for grace. Even during the Fall, God had made provision by His grace.

Mephibosheth was unable to care for even his basic necessities such as bathing and providing food for himself. He had to be carried wherever he went because he could not walk. The story goes on to tell us Mephibosheth was taken in and cared for by a wealthy man who lived in LoDebar. LoDebar means "pastureless" and speaks of a barren land. So, here was a boy born to royalty, living at the mercy of a wealthy landowner, in a barren place.

Labeled

In several scriptures that refer to him, it states, *Mephibosheth, who was lame in his feet.* It is as if his lameness was the identifying factor of his life. He was "labeled" – LAME.

Many of God's people today live with places of "lameness" that may not show on the outside. Their walk has been hindered by the wounds they've experienced in life. They live with labels from the past:

You know Barb, she's the one who's been divorced twice...
Jim, the man you can never depend on...
Mary, the one who was abused...

Even though they may have found grace to be healed, many find themselves living in a barren place, with the "lameness" and labels of the past defining who they are. Like Mephibosheth, they, too, were born to royalty. They need their King to come and recognize them for who they truly are, just as David did for Mephibosheth.

In his desire to honor his covenant with his friend, Jonathan, David called for any descendants that were still alive from the house of Saul. Mephibosheth was brought to him. Listen to the shame in Mephibosheth's heart as he approached David: *What is your servant that you should look upon such a dead dog as I?* (2 Samuel 9:8). The phrase "dead dog" signified a person of no value. But David looks beyond the lameness and sees the heritage of a king.

Promises

David makes 3 promises to Mephibosheth (2 Samuel 9:1-13).

Restore:

> *[I] will restore to you all the land of Saul your grandfather...*
> (2 Samuel 9:7)

David would give back to Mephibosheth all that was taken from him – his inheritance.

Just as our King restores what the enemy has taken from us:

> *Instead of their shame, my people will receive a double portion,*
> *And instead of disgrace, they will rejoice in their inheritance;*
> *And so they will inherit a double portion in their land,*
> *And everlasting joy will be theirs* (Isaiah 61:7 NIV).

Sustain:

> *...you shall eat bread at my table continually* (2 Samuel 9:7).

Mephibosheth would no longer lack sustenance.

Just as our King provides all we need:

> *And Jesus said to them, I am the bread of life. He who comes to Me shall never hunger, and he who believes in Me shall never thirst* (John 6:35-36).

And in Psalm 23:1

> *The Lord is my shepherd; I shall not want.*

Regain:

> *...like one of the king's sons* (2 Samuel 9:11).

Mephibosheth regains his true identity as a part of the king's family. Our King paid the price to redeem our true identity as part of God's royal family.

> *...having predestined us to adoption as sons by Jesus Christ to Himself, according to the good pleasure of His will, to the praise of the glory of His grace, by which He made us accepted in the Beloved. In Him we have redemption through His blood...* (Ephesians 1:5-7)

> *For this reason, I bow my knees to the Father of our Lord Jesus Christ, from whom the whole family in heaven and earth is named...*Ephesians (3:14-15)

The beautiful story of Mephibosheth, whose name means "Dispeller of Shame," shows us David as a type of our King, Jesus, who comes to us in our lameness, our forsakenness (shame) and desolation (barrenness), to redeem, restore, and bring us to our Father's table so that we may enjoy the Bread of Life forever.

The strongest antidote for shame is a revelation of God's love for you personally. I'm convinced it was knowing and experiencing God's love firsthand that enabled David to give it freely to Mephibosheth. God's unconditional love made David a man after God's own heart.

Healed to Serve

In the Old Testament system of sacrifices, an animal who was lame was disqualified from being used as an offering (Leviticus 22:20-23). Similarly, the descendants of Aaron who were lame were considered unfit for service (Leviticus 21:16-21). As a nation of priests and kings (1 Peter 2:9, Revelation 1:6), we are to be living sacrifices (Romans 12:1), and for that reason, it is crucial that we allow God to both reveal, and then heal, the places of lameness in our lives. His unconditional love and acceptance will bring wholeness that we may serve Him and make Him known.

Matthew 5:48 (The Message):
In a word, what I'm saying is, Grow up. You're kingdom subjects. Now live like it. Live out your God-created identity. Live generously and graciously toward others, the way God lives toward you.

Let's Talk About It

1. Can you relate to the terms, "forsaken" and "desolate?" In what ways?
2. How has the enemy used the lie to weave "tangled threads" into your life?
3. Identify specific areas where the enemy has caused you to feel "you are not enough."

At Home This Week

1. Give the Holy Spirit permission to show you where you have been entangled in the lie. Then make a choice – a commitment in prayer – to no longer live in the lie, but to live in the power of the truth.
2. Meditate on Ephesians, chapter one. Ask the Holy Spirit to quicken to your heart those verses He wants to weave into the fabric of your being.

Truth to Embrace

1. The enemy of our souls would like nothing better than to hold the church captive to the system he has deceptively set in place in the world.
2. God is able to heal the most broken of his children and fully unravel all the tangled threads.

DISCOLORED THREADS

As I mentioned in the previous chapter, the enemy comes to distort and even destroy our identity. Using a variety of deceptions to communicate his lie, they become discolored threads in the tapestry of our life. Let me highlight a few.

Words

Proverbs 18:21 states, *Death and life are in the power of the tongue.* Often, we fail to realize the power of our words. Parents, teachers, siblings, and peers say things that can affect our identity. Counselors' files are filled with stories of people who had negative words spoken over their lives as youngsters, only to watch the fulfillment walked out in their adult lives. Words such as, "You'll never amount to anything," "Why can't you get good grades like your sister/ brother?" have the capacity to communicate a message that impacts the very identity of a child. Words become beliefs, and beliefs direct our lives.

Words also have the power to impart life and blessing in a person's life. God's Word is able to heal our misshapen self-perception and impart truth about who we are.

Psalm 107:20: *He sent His word and healed them.*

Looks

Did you know that a look expressing approval or disapproval can impact our self-concept? Looks, or facial expressions, convey an attitude of the heart. Much of what we communicate is not so much in the words we say, but in other means of communication: body language, tone of voice, feelings, and attitudes.

When I was in third grade, I proudly came to school one day with a new pair of shoes that I thought were wonderful. At one point, I had to go up to the teacher's desk. When I did, my teacher looked at me, looked down at my shoes, looked at me again, and turned her head away. I was crushed. The look of disapproval on her face was such that I never felt acceptable in that classroom for the rest of the school year.

Even a look can affect our identity. God looks at us with eyes of love.

Psalm 33:13-16
The LORD looks from heaven; He sees all the sons of men.
From the place of His dwelling, He looks on all the inhabitants of the earth;
He fashions their hearts individually; He considers all their works.

The Word also tells us that the Lord guides us with His eye (Psalm 32:8).

Touch

Touch can impact our identity. There are loving, nurturing kinds of touch that communicate love, acceptance, warmth, security, and trust. There are also inappropriate kinds of touch that do untold damage to the identity of a child. Abuse distorts a person's self-concept at the very core of their being, which is why it is so destructive. It not only harms the physical body, it ravages the soul.

I once ministered to a woman who had been so devastated by abuse, that she could not even say the words, "Jesus loves me" until we had prayed and ministered to her for several minutes.

Jesus longs to touch us by His Holy Spirit and heal the devastation in our lives.

Luke 6:19: *And the whole multitude sought to touch Him, for power went out from Him and healed them all.*

Neglect

Physical and emotional neglect, abandonment, lack of nurturing, all impact a person's identity. The absence of needed care, whether deliberate or unintentional, is just as damaging to the identity of a child as abuse. It can leave one with a sense of incompleteness, emptiness, and worthlessness, just as a missed stitch in a tapestry mars the beauty of the work.

These missing pieces lead to a lifetime of seeking to fill the empty places in unfulfilling ways. God wants to fill those places that have been left void through neglect and abandonment.

Psalm 27:10: *When my father and my mother forsake me, Then the LORD will take care of me.*

The word translated "care" is a Hebrew word meaning "to cure, recover, put everything together."[10] God's restoration heals the places of "lameness" in our lives.

Cultural Messages

There are nations in the world where a person's value depends upon gender. Little girls are of no consequence. As a result, they are not given even the basic necessities of food and clothing if it means a little boy will go without.

In his book, *Why Not Women?*, Loren Cunningham, founder of Youth With A Mission (YWAM), notes that "450 million women are physically impaired due to childhood malnutrition. In many societies, girls and their mothers eat only after the men and boys are fed."[11]

In Afghanistan, under the Taliban, women suffer greatly. The law forbids the education of females and prohibits women from working outside the home. Those without husbands to support them have no means of livelihood. Women are isolated from the world and literally become prisoners in their own homes. Before the Taliban's rule, many women attended universities, were highly educated, and held prestigious positions as doctors and lawyers.

Mr. Cunningham recounts an experience he had on an airplane as he flew into the capital of one of the most restrictive Middle Eastern nations. When the Swiss Air flight left Zurich, all the men and women were dressed in Western clothing. As the plane neared its final destination, the women began disappearing into the restrooms to emerge covered from head to foot in "abayas" – thick, black clothing covering them from head to foot.

Mr. Cunningham states:
The women had no faces. They had no identity. They were just anonymous figures shrouded in black.[12]

There are cultures in which a woman is looked on as nothing more than a piece of property to be used at the discretion of the owner (her husband). There are religions that teach women that they are inferior to men intellectually, spiritually, and in every other way. The identity of millions of women throughout the world has been destroyed through the lie that the enemy has disseminated through culture and religion.

Even in Western culture, we receive messages daily about what it means to be a woman or a man. Standards are set through the media, magazines, radio and TV, movies, the fashion world. Case in point: in the 1950s, the epitome of female beauty was the full-figured Marilyn Monroe. Did you know Marilyn wore a size 14 dress?!

One decade later, a tall British model, aptly named Twiggy, set a whole new standard of female beauty. Her stick-like figure was a radical departure from the curvy, full figure of the 1950s. We've been living under that 60's image ever since!

Men receive cultural messages that affect their identity as well. "Real men don't cry" or show emotion. Sports figures are held up as role models to emulate. What does that say to the boy who is not athletic? Think of all the cultural messages we receive every day that establish a standard most men and women can never live up to.

These are just a few of the deceptions through which the enemy seeks to negatively impact our identity. The result? We live out of a distorted or unclear image of who we are, instead of who God created us to be.

Rick Joyner, founder of MorningStar Ministries and recognized prophetic voice in the body of Christ, stated:

One reason for the explosive increase of lawlessness and suicide that we are seeing in the emerging generation is because they lack a clear identity and purpose. Because we were created for the Lord and to have fellowship with God who is Spirit, we can never find true peace or fulfillment until we are walking in our purpose in the Lord.[13]

The Master Weaver

God, in His infinite wisdom and unfailing love, pulls all the discolored and tangled threads the enemy and the world have sewn into our lives, and begins to weave His truth, His purpose, and His design into us. The enemy's plan to distort, destroy and diminish the image of God in us will never succeed as long as we open our hearts to the Holy Spirit and allow the unraveling to take place so that restoration can come. Proverbs 21:30 (NIV) assures us that, *there is no wisdom, no insight, no plan that can succeed against the LORD.*

Let's Talk About It

1. Can you identify the "discolored threads" the enemy has used to distort your identity? Share one or two experiences.
2. Are you ready to disentangle yourself from the lie and come into the power of the truth about who you are in Christ?
3. Pray one for another, committing yourself to the work of the "Master Weaver" as He unravels threads that were not of His choosing and begins to weave new ones in their place.

At Home This Week

1. We have identified 5 specific ways in which the enemy communicates his lie to us. Interestingly, in their book, *The Blessing*, Gary Smalley and John Trent[14] identify five parts of parental blessing intended to impart God's love and identity into a person's life. They are listed below. Meditate on each one, asking your heavenly Father to express His blessing to your heart.

   • Meaningful touch – warm and nurturing physical touch (God can touch your spirit and soul).
   • Spoken word – words of affirmation, blessing, love, acceptance, and encouragement (through His Word and His people).
   • Expressing high value – acknowledging the intrinsic worth and value of the person (He can give understanding of your value in Him).
   • Picturing a special future – expressing hope for the future (His plan and destiny for your life).
   • An active commitment – a commitment to helping the person realize their full identity and destiny in the Lord. (His commitment to you is unending – Phil 1:6).

Truth to Embrace

1. Much of what we communicate is not so much in the words we say, but in other means of communication: body language, tone of voice, feelings, and attitude.
2. There are nations in the world where a person's value depends upon gender. Little girls are of no consequence.
3. *There is no wisdom, no insight, no plan that can succeed against the Lord* (Proverbs 21:30).

WORLDLY DESIGNS

I mentioned in Chapter One that within each one of us is a deep need for security and significance. These two elements shape our identity and can be fulfilled only in God.

Often, life's painful experiences make it difficult to believe that God would love us unconditionally and that He has a purpose for our life. Longing to fill the void inside, we embrace the third part of the lie, "you need something from the world to make you enough." We look for love, value, and acceptance in all the wrong places. We turn to the world to satisfy our need and to define who we are.

1 John 2:15 : *Do not love the world or the things in the world. If anyone loves the world, the love of the Father is not in him.*

We typically think of this scripture in terms of material things or overt acts of sin. However, loving the world also means accepting the world's system of determining our value. The enemy has constructed the world's system in such a way that it will always leave us feeling like we don't measure up in one or many ways. Let me share a few of the places the enemy leads us to believe we will find identity and value.

Accomplishments

In Luke 10, we read the account of Jesus sending seventy of his disciples on a short-term mission trip. He gave explicit instructions on what luggage to take (none!) (v. 4), how to greet potential recipients of their ministry (v. 5), how to handle honorariums (v. 7-8), and exactly how to minister (v. 9). He even told them how to deal with rejection (v. 10-12). It seems it was a successful mission trip because the seventy returned excited over the fact that the demons were subject to them (v. 17).

What a sense of power must have come from accomplishing such ministerial exploits! Jesus' response? He reminded them that the real cause for rejoicing was that their names were written in the Book of Life – more important than what they did, was who they were!

How easy it is for us to define ourselves by the things we have accomplished. There is a fine line between the sense of satisfaction that comes from knowing you are following God's will and using your gifts, and striving for accomplishment in order to feel accepted and valued.

One of the ways you can sometimes distinguish between the two is to ask yourself this question: How important is it that others know what I have accomplished? It's not wrong to take joy in a job well done, as long as it is not the source of your identity.

Mike Bickle, pastor and founder of the House of Prayer, in Kansas City, MO, stated that God wants us to be relationally oriented first and achievement oriented second.[15] Yes, we are to fulfill the Great Commission, but who we are in Him is far more important than what we do for Him. In fact, who we are will impact what we do.

Performance

In his book, *The Search for Significance*, Robert McGee formulates the world's equation for finding identity:

Self-Worth = Performance + Others' Opinions.[16]

How well we perform and please others determine how we feel about ourselves. This is a trap that causes us to struggle continually to live up to a certain standard. Performance orientation can lead to perfectionism: everything must be done flawlessly. Driven from the inside to achieve success on the outside, it is often rooted in a fear of failing. Failure produces feelings of worthlessness and unacceptability. Nothing less than perfect will do.

We listen to the negative voices that urge us to prove our worth by doing something relevant, spectacular, powerful. To experience the love and respect we crave, we must earn it! Second-best will never do. Drivenness. That strategy may seem to work for a time, but the result is ultimately unfulfilling and doesn't satisfy.

Success is not final, failure is not fatal: it is the courage to continue that counts (Winston Churchill).

Wrong Belief

Because of this wrong belief that our value is based on how well we perform, we often approach our relationship with God from a performance base. Have you ever felt distanced from God because you were not spending enough time reading the Bible, or praying? Have you ever felt God was mad at you because you failed to resist a temptation? God does not respond to our performance, He responds to our heart.

No Clipboard

God doesn't have a giant clipboard with a checklist of chores He expects us to perform before we can enter His presence. He invites us into His presence freely with open arms, eager to be with us.

Several years ago, when my grandson was about two years old, I was driving home from work one night thinking about seeing him when I arrived. Anyone who's been around two-year-olds knows they are not perfect! My grandson was no exception. As I drove home, it seemed the traffic lights took longer than usual, the cars in front of me moved slower…I was so anxious to see him. I could see myself walking in the front door, greeted by his smile and outstretched arms, waiting to be picked up. My heart was warmed at the thought.

In that moment, the Lord spoke to my heart saying, *The way you feel about Zach is just how I feel about you. I can't wait to be with you and spend time together.* I've learned something else about time with my Father: it doesn't have to be long, protracted periods of time, although those are good, too. Even a few moments, giving Him my full attention, telling Him I love Him, delights His heart and mine.

A two-year-old won't stay in your arms for very long before he's wiggling to run and play, but, oh, those few moments of holding him close! What joy it brought to my heart. That's how your Father feels about you!

Position or Title

Deriving a sense of value from a position or title, whether in business or ministry, is looking for identity in the wrong places.

Many have relied so heavily on their position or title that if it is taken away, their sense of value plummets. The business world applauds a mindset that encourages people to "climb the corporate ladder." Unfortunately, many reach the top only to find it doesn't meet the need they thought it would. It turns out to be one of those threads that seem to go nowhere!

Desire to be Above Others

Even two of Jesus' closest disciples, James and John, experienced this need. Although they were part of His inner circle, they longed to have a special position with Him for all eternity. *Grant us that we may sit, one on Your right and the other on Your left in Your glory* (Mark 10:37).

Needing to have a distinguished title or position is wanting to be above others. Rather than fostering unity, it can create relational problems. Read the account of this incident to see how the other ten disciples reacted to James' and John's request. They were not pleased!

Along a similar line is deriving a sense of value or importance by being close to someone in a highly visible position or a place of authority. Being close to those "at the top" lends a false sense of significance. This need is obvious in those in the habit of "name dropping."

Psalm 4:3 states, *But know that the LORD has set apart **for Himself** [emphasis added] him who is godly.* He has not set us apart for a job, a position, or even a ministry. He has first set us apart for Himself, for intimate relationship with Him.

Education, Intelligence

Some define themselves by the letters that follow their name, such as Ph.D., or the number of degrees they hold. While I strongly believe that education is vital and can help lead to a fulfilling life, our value is not dependent on academic accomplishments.

Henri Nouwen, one of the great spiritual writers of our day, is a beautiful example of a person who possessed all the accolades academia had to offer. He authored over 25 books, taught at the University of Notre Dame, Yale, and Harvard, and lectured around the world. The last several years of his life were spent serving as a pastor in a community of mentally disabled people. There he found the true meaning and value of life among a group of people who were not impressed by his academic accomplishments. He learned that the people he had gone to help were the very ones who taught him the most.

1 Corinthians 8:1: *Knowledge puffs up, but love edifies.*

Gifts or Talents

Do you ever find a sense of value in being known as a prophet, a skilled intercessor, leader, or teacher? As we'll see in Chapter Nine, it is important to know our gifting and use the God-given gifts and abilities to advance His kingdom, but we cannot derive our identity from our gifts.

Unless we know who we are in Him and have allowed Him to develop His character in us, even His gifts can become a snare to us (see 1 Corinthians 13:1-10). It has been said that character is God's inoculation against His awesome power flowing through mere human beings.

There are many other things we could list through which we try to find acceptance and value, such as physical appearance, money, possessions, fame, or recognition, but one of the avenues we seek identity most is through other people.

People

Every person in our life has the potential to weave a thread into our tapestry, a thread that distorts or a thread that enhances.

Parents

Beginning with our family, the words of parents, as well as their hopes and dreams for us, can affect our identity.

Relationships are the fabric of our life. We feel like a whole person when all the pieces are in their proper place. Sometimes there are small rips in the family fabric but they're patched or sewn up and you go on. But when a significant member of the family isn't there, or isn't who they should be, the entire fabric of the family is torn, often from top to bottom. Mother and Father are significant members. The empty place in our life can be carried for years.[17]

Have you ever known someone who pursued a particular career, such as a doctor, lawyer, or politician, because it was the desire of his or her parent(s)? Some children grow up with expectations that they will continue the family business, or be in ministry like their parents, grandparents, and even great-grandparents before them. Until a few short decades ago, most little girls grew up believing that their only identity as adults would be that of a wife and mother. Parental influence can be either a positive or negative force in helping to shape our identity. To reach adulthood only to find the plans and goals were those of the parents can negatively impact a person and can trigger an identity crisis. However, parental encouragement of the potential gift in their child can strengthen and affirm the child's unique identity.

Others

There are others who influence our identity: spouses, relatives, teachers, siblings, peers, employers, etc. In their struggle for independence, teens will often reject their parents' opinion but conform to the standard set by their peers. As adults, we may so admire someone that we try to be like them or strive for their approval.

A note in the Life Recovery Bible states it clearly:

Many of us have spent our lives trying to be someone we are not… Maybe we have difficulty accepting our personality, our appearance, our handicaps, even our talents. Perhaps we spend our energy and time trying to be what someone else wants us to be because we feel that who we are is not enough.[18]

When we attempt to find our identity in what someone else thinks of us, we are looking to that person for a sense of respect and dignity.

Clothed With Beauty

(He) redeems your life from the pit and corruption; (He) beautifies, dignifies, and crowns you with loving-kindness and tender mercies (Psalm 103:4 AMP).

Dignity is the quality of being worthy of esteem or honor.

It means stateliness, proper pride and self-respect.[19] The dignity we long for will never will be found in the esteem of other people. Only through knowing who we are in Him, and more importantly, who He is in us, will we find our true worth. In looking to people, we sabotage the very way to true dignity, esteem, honor, and self-respect.

Psalm 103:4 pictures God clothing us with beauty and dignity. Other people can't clothe us with those qualities. The best they can do is cover us with a brash, garish beauty, like a costume or clothing fad that quickly loses its attraction. Just as a fashion fad comes and goes leaving you shopping for the next new item, you find you need constant affirmation in order to feel good about yourself. It is one of the ways we give our identity over to others and allow them to define us. Only God can clothe us with the beauty and dignity we long for. It is not an outward beauty, but an inward, eternal quality that will never fade or go out of style.

1 Peter 3:3-5:

Do not let your adornment be merely outward—arranging the hair, wearing gold, or putting on fine apparel—rather let it be the hidden person of the heart, with the incorruptible beauty of a gentle and quiet spirit, which is very precious in the sight of God.

I like the way one author describes the challenge before us:

You are questing for wholeness and a healthy autonomy from the expectations of others.[20]

Let's Talk About It

1. Have you pursued any of the "worldly designs" mentioned in this chapter? Which ones?
2. Are there certain people in your life, such as authority figures (parents, teachers, employers, etc.), whose acceptance and approval are necessary for you to feel good about yourself? Name them and explain why their opinion is so important to you.
3. The world's equation for finding identity is:
   Self Worth = Performance + Others' Opinions.
   Based on the truth of God's Word, formulate a new equation for your identity.

At Home This Week

1. Focus your prayer this week on asking God to show you the ways you pursue "worldly designs" or ways you look to the world to make you feel you are valuable and worthwhile.
2. Expect the Holy Spirit to quicken "worldly designs" to your mind in situations you encounter throughout the week.
3. Purpose to respond to each circumstance based on God's truth about your identity, not the enemy's or the world's.

Truth to Embrace

1. Only God can clothe us with the beauty and dignity we long for. It is not an outward beauty, but an inward, eternal quality that will never fade or go out of style.
2. God doesn't have a giant clipboard with a checklist of chores He expects us to accomplish before we can enter His presence.
3. The Lord tells us that who we are in Him is far more important than what we do for Him.

BROKEN THREADS

Looking for love in all the wrong places results in broken threads. When we live from a distorted or unclear identity and subsequently look for something from the world to make us feel worthwhile, relational challenges can result. If we really knew in our hearts who we are in God – that is, experienced His unconditional, unfailing love for us personally, and knew His plan for our life – some of the following issues would be minimized, perhaps even non-existent. Let me share a few with you.

Comparison

Not being at peace with who we are in God leads to comparing ourselves to one another. If we compare ourselves to other parts of God's tapestry, or try to look like other "stitches," we deprive God and the world of the color, texture, and design that is in us. Relationally, comparison puts people on different "levels" and we interact with them accordingly.

People you deem to be more mature or gifted than you, may cause you to feel inferior or intimidated. You may not feel free to express your perspective. Others, who may not be as mature as you, or who do not have the knowledge or experience you have, can cause you to feel superior. In that case, you might not be open to hear what they have to offer or share.

Comparing doesn't allow you to relate to others on a person-to-person, heart-to-heart basis, so the relationship is less than genuine. It can also keep you from using your gifts as effectively as you might. Silenced by intimidation, the portion you bring remains hidden. The Word says it is not wise to compare ourselves one to another (2 Corinthians 10:12).

Competition

Comparing can lead to competing. You feel a need to prove yourself, to show that you are just as capable as the one to whom you are comparing yourself. You want to impress the person. While competition in athletic endeavors may produce champions, in the context of Christian relationships, it is deadly. Instead of working together, we work against each other in order to come out on top. We can't have open, trusting relationships when we are competing with one another. Strife and division are the result.

Mark 9:33-35

Then He came to Capernaum. And when He was in the house He asked them, "What was it you disputed among yourselves on the road?" But they kept silent, for on the road they had disputed among themselves who would be the greatest. And He sat down, called the twelve, and said to them, "If anyone desires to be first, he shall be last of all and servant of all."

Self-Promotion

If you feel you lack the recognition you deserve, you may tend to promote yourself to receive affirmation. You want people to know how successful (or gifted or intelligent or talented) you are so that you can feel good about yourself.

James 3:13-18 (HCSB)

Who is wise and has understanding among you? He should show his works by good conduct with wisdom's gentleness. But if you have bitter envy and selfish ambition in your heart, don't brag and deny the truth. Such wisdom does not come from above but is earthly, unspiritual, demonic. For where envy and selfish ambition exist, there is disorder and every kind of evil. But the wisdom from above is first pure, then peace-loving, gentle, compliant, full of mercy and good fruits, without favoritism and hypocrisy. And the fruit of righteousness is sown in peace by those who cultivate peace.

Covetousness

Living with a self-perception that is distorted by shame and reproach can breed the sin of covetousness. Covetousness, simply put, is longing to be in someone else's situation or to have what they have. It can be jealousy over a friend's happy marriage or envying the material success of another.

In ministry, it can mean wanting the anointing or gifts of a brother or sister. In essence, it is being discontent with what you have or who you are.

Hebrews 13:5

Let your conduct be without covetousness; be content with such things as you have.

For He Himself has said, "I will never leave you nor forsake you."

Luke 12:15
And He said to them, "Take heed and beware of covetousness, for one's life does not consist in the abundance of the things he possesses."

Judging

Jesus said, *Judge not, that you be not judged; For with what judgment you judge, you will be judged*; (Matthew 7:1-2).

The word, "judge," means to condemn, criticize, or punish. One of the primary reasons we judge is because we do not feel the security of unconditional love.

Henri Nouwen expresses it beautifully:
Can we free ourselves from the need to judge others? Yes…by claiming for ourselves the truth that we are the beloved daughters and sons of God.

As long as we continue to live as if we are what we do, what we have, and what other people think about us, we will remain filled with judgments, opinions, evaluations, and condemnations. We will remain addicted to the need to put people and things in their "right" place.

To the degree that we embrace the truth that our identity is not rooted in our success, power, or popularity, but in God's infinite love, to that degree can we let go of our need to judge.[21]

Concluding Truth

What can we conclude from this chapter? That the lie of the enemy that drives us to seek our identity in the things the world has to offer will never satisfy the deep longing in our hearts. By its very design, it leaves us empty and continually running after more success, more affirmation, more recognition.

I'm reminded of the "black holes" scientists have discovered in space. A black hold is a region of space in which the gravitational pull is so powerful that nothing, not even light, can escape. They are like bottomless chasms that can never be filled. Our hearts can be like those "black holes"…try as we might, we can never fill them with earthly sources of fulfillment.

The reality is that those earthly sources become idols in our lives, occupying the place in our hearts designed to be held by the One who made us. Only God's limitless love can satisfy our need for security. Only God's purpose for us can give meaning and significance to our life.

Ephesians 1:11

It's in Christ that we find out who we are and what we're living for. Long before we first heard of Christ and got our hopes up, he had his eye on us, had designs on us for glorious living, part of the overall purpose he is working out in everything and everyone (The Message).

A strong self-concept founded in God's love results in peace in our hearts, fulfillment in our lives, and healthy relationships. It provides a secure base from which to deepen our intimacy with God and relate to others in honesty, transparency, and vulnerability.

When we are confident in who we are in Him, we are free to take responsibility for our beliefs, emotions, attitudes, and behavior, without fear or condemnation. We can allow others to be responsible for their actions without feeling guilty or responsible for how they feel. Healthy boundaries can be established that will diminish the need for damaging behavior such as manipulation and control.

You are free to relate to others as co-laborers, joint heirs, peers, instead of being on different levels. You are free to take the place God has designed for you in His body without worrying about what others are called to do. Do you remember when Peter asked Jesus about John's future (John 21:22)? Jesus replied, *If I will that he remain till I come, what is that to you? You follow Me.* In other words, embrace what I've called YOU to, and live in obedience to Me.

Let's Talk About It

1. What relational behaviors can you relate to as "broken threads" in your life?
2. What relational damage has resulted from these wrong choices?
3. Describe how you might relate to someone if you were certain that you were completely accepted and deeply love by them. Do you have such a relationship in your life with another person? With God?

At Home This Week

Read through the book of Proverbs, listing verses that identify where your true security and significance are found.

Truth to Embrace

1. Comparing doesn't allow you to relate to others on a person-to-person, heart-to-heart basis, so the relationship is less than genuine.
2. By its very design, the lie of the enemy will leave us empty and continually running after more success.
3. A strong self-concept founded in God's love results in peace in our hearts, fulfillment in our lives, and healthy relationships.

THREADS OF PURPOSE

When God fashioned us, He placed within each one special abilities, gifts and talents, natural and spiritual, that He desires to use for His glory. Our heavenly Father, *from Whom comes every good gift and every perfect gift* (James 1:17), has given us spiritual gifts that are meant to help us know and fulfill, our part in His overall plan and purpose in the earth. Because no one else is created quite like you, with the unique blend of personality, gifts, talents, and abilities, there is no one else on earth that can fulfill your place in God's plan. Knowing the gifts He has placed within you, will be strong clues to your destiny in God. Let's take a brief look at spiritual gifts in the Bible.

Now concerning spiritual gifts, brethren, I do not want you to be ignorant: (1 Corinthians 12:1)

The Amplified Bible says it this way:

Now about the spiritual gifts (the special endowments of supernatural energy), brethren, I do not want you to be misinformed.

Not only are we to be knowledgeable about the spiritual gifts God has given us, but we are to pursue them: *But earnestly desire the best gifts* (1 Corinthians 12:31).

"Earnestly desire" means to covet earnestly, to pursue, to strive after. [22]

First of all, DISCOVER what your gifts are if you are not already aware of them (Rom. 12:1-3, Matt. 7:7-8, James 1:5).

Secondly, be willing to DEVELOP your gifts (1 Timothy 4:14a, 2 Timothy 1:6).

Thirdly, DEPLOY, or exercise your gifts (1 Peter 4:10, Matthew 25:14-30), for the strengthening of the body of Christ. Understanding how you are gifted also helps you to better understand others who have different gifts and whose ministry may look very different from yours.

Three Categories of Gifts

There are three listings of gifts in the Bible.

Motivational Gifts – Romans 12:4-8
Ministry or Office Gifts – Ephesians 4:7-13
Manifestation Gifts or Holy Spirit Gifts – 1 Corinthians 12:8-11

Within the three categories of spiritual gifts listed in the Bible, we find:

The gifts of the Father – MOTIVATIONAL GIFTS – foundational, creation gifts, inherent in the believer. Romans 12:4-8: Prophecy, Serving, Teaching, Exhortation, Giving, Administration, Mercy.

The gifts of the Son – MINISTRY GIFTS – given for the equipping of the saints and the ongoing work of the ministry. Ephesians 4:7-13: apostle, prophet, evangelist, pastor, teacher.

The gifts of the Holy Spirit – MANIFESTATION GIFTS – available and operative for all believers for the building up and edification of the church. 1 Corinthians 12:8-11: word of wisdom, word of knowledge, discerning of spirits, faith, gifts of healings, working of miracles, prophecy, tongues, interpretation of tongues.

All of these gifts, while diverse, are given by one Spirit. They come from the greatest gift – the Holy Spirit – and are visible evidence of His presence and activity in a believer's life.

In Paul's discussion of the Motivational Gifts, LOVE is emphasized (Romans 12:9-10,18,21).

In Paul's discussion of the Ministry Gifts, LOVE is emphasized (Ephesians 4:2-3,15-16).

In Paul's discussion of the Manifestation Gifts, LOVE is emphasized (1 Corinthians 13).

LOVE is to be the basis from which all gifts are to be exercised!

Because we are created in His image, every person has a spiritual gift, or more accurately, a mix of spiritual gifts. No one has all the gifts, but rather a combination of several, with one or two being dominant. The Bible likens the body of Christ to a physical body Romans 12:5-6 and 1 Corinthians 12:20-30. The significance of this image is that it shows us we need each other. Your gifts make up for the ones I lack and my gifts do the same for you. God intends us to be interdependent with each other – not dependent nor independent, but interdependent.

In this chapter, we will deal more fully with the Motivational Gifts because they relate to our identity and who we are. They "move" us because they are part of our spiritual DNA. The Ministry Gifts and Manifestation Gifts relate more to our function in the body of Christ, or what we do, so we will just give a brief overview. For more information on these two categories of gifts, see the resources listed at the end of this book.

MOTIVATIONAL GIFTS

What do we mean by "Motivational Gifts"? These are spiritual gifts that motivate, or inspire, or cause us to respond to life in a certain way. They are part of the way God "wired" us when He created us. For that reason, a teacher will approach a situation differently than someone gifted in mercy. As we look at the gifts and the characteristics, strengths, and weaknesses of each, hopefully you will be able to identity the gifts that are part of the way God made you.

Prophecy/Perceiver

More aptly call the gift of perceiving, it has also been called the "insight" gift.
The Greek word, *propheteia*, means "the speaking forth of the mind and counsel of God."[23] As a motivational gift, it is the special ability given by the Father that enables a person to view life and circumstances with spiritual insight given by God.

The motivation of the Perceiver is:
- To clearly perceive the will and counsel of God, to seek out the truth
- Uncover hindrances to spiritual growth so people can get right with God

The Perceiver believes growth occurs by becoming aware of the sin in the heart, then repenting. They focus on spiritual principles and the fulfillment of God's plan.

The need met in the body of Christ: SPIRITUAL

Characteristics (Strengths)
- Able to see past the outward to the inner motives of the heart
- Focus is on the eternal rather than temporal
- Tends to be strong, opinionated, black and white, strong sense of right and wrong
- Strict personal standards, lives life in a godly manner

Potential Pitfalls (Weaknesses)
- Focusing on the negative instead of the positive
- Can be judgmental and critical, especially of self
- Painfully blunt

Examples of Perceivers in Scripture:
    Anna (Luke 2:36-38), John the Baptist (Luke 3:1-22, Matthew :1-17)

Favorite scripture of the Perceiver: Proverbs 28:13
    A man who refuses to admit his mistakes can never be successful. But if he confesses and forsakes them, he gets another chance. (The Living Bible)

Serving/Ministry

This gift is the special ability God gives to minister to the needs of others. The Greek word, *diakonian*, means serving or "ministering."[24]

The motivation of the Server is to:
- Demonstrate love by meeting practical needs (i.e., food, shelter, comfort)
- Lend practical assistance to those in need

The need met in the body: PRACTICAL

Characteristics (Strengths)
- Genuine love for others is expressed in deeds and actions
- Gives of self, time, and assets to meet the need
- Quick to identify and anticipate needs and then faithful and diligent to meet them
- Tends to be supportive of leadership

Potential Pitfalls (Weaknesses)
- Can be overcommitted, unable to say "no" to the neglect of their own family
- Easily hurt or resentful when not appreciated
- Critical of others who don't see and meet obvious needs

Examples of Servers in Scripture:
    Martha (Luke 10:38-42, John 11:1-40, 12:2), Stephen (Acts 6:1-4)

Favorite scripture of the Server: Matthew 25:35-40
    For I was hungry, and you fed me. I was thirsty, and you gave me a drink. I was a stranger, and you invited me into your home. I was naked, and you

gave me clothing. I was sick, and you cared for me. I was in prison, and you visited me.'

Then these righteous ones will reply, 'Lord, when did we ever see you hungry and feed you? Or thirsty and give you something to drink? Or a stranger and show you hospitality? Or naked and give you clothing? When did we ever see you sick or in prison and visit you?'

And the King will say, 'I tell you the truth, when you did it to one of the least of these my brothers and sisters, you were doing it to me.' (NLT)

Teaching

This gift is the special ability God gives to be able to communicate truth in a way that is easy to understand and apply. The Greek word, *didasko*, means "to teach"[25] or "to give instruction."[26]

The motivation of the Teacher is to:
- Search out and validate truth and impart that knowledge to others
- Motivate others to consistently and enthusiastically study the Bible and assimilate its truth

The need met in the body is: MENTAL

Characteristics (Strengths)
- Loves to learn, enjoys Bible study and research, validates truth from the Word
- Presents truth in a way that is easily understood and applied, using illustrations from the Bible and presenting a comprehensive picture of the topic
- Uneasy with subjective truth – begins with scripture and relates it to personal experience
- Very conscientious about teaching the truth and not being in error

Potential Pitfalls (Weaknesses)
- "Knowledge puffs up" – can take credit for intelligence and knowledge gained through study
- Can be argumentative in an effort to know all the facts or because they don't accept another's teaching – can be critical of other teachers
- Need to verify every statement by scripture, hindering wider applications of the Word

Examples of Teachers in Scripture: Mary (Luke 10:39, John 11:45), Apollos (Acts 18:24-28, 1 Corinthians 3:6)

Favorite scripture of the Teacher: 2 Timothy 2:15

Study and be eager and do your utmost to present yourself to God approved (tested by trial), a workman who has no cause to be ashamed, correctly analyzing and accurately dividing [rightly handling and skillfully teaching] the Word of Truth (AMP).

Exhortation

This gift is "the special ability God gives to certain members of the Body of Christ to minister words of comfort, consolation, encouragement, and counsel to other members of the Body of Christ in such a way that they feel helped and healed."[27]

The Greek word, *parakaleo*, means "to come alongside of" or "a calling to one's own side."[28] It is the same Greek root from which we get the word, *Parakletos*: a term referring to the Holy Spirit, who comes alongside us as Comforter and Counselor.

The motivation of the Exhorter is to:
- Encourage individuals to grow and mature spiritually
- Focus on meeting the personal psychological needs of the body through edifying, encouraging, and challenging
- Keep us aware of the importance of applying spiritual truth to our daily walk

The need met in the body: PERSONAL

Characteristics (Strengths)
- Enjoys counseling and encouraging people to grow, whether one-on-one, or through teaching or speaking
- Gains insight through experience and validates it with Scripture
- Accepts others where they are, non-judgmental
- See trials and conflict as positive – an opportunity for growth

Potential Pitfalls (Weaknesses)
- Can become frustrated or impatient when people don't change
- Use scriptures out of context in order to make a point
- Can be too outspoken, independent, or overly self-confident

Examples of Exhorters in Scripture:
Deborah (Judges 4, 5), Barnabas (Acts 4:36; 11:23-26)

Favorite scripture of the Exhorter: Proverbs 25:11-12
Timely advice is lovely, like golden apples in a silver basket.
To one who listens, valid criticism is like a gold earring or other gold jewelry (NLT).

Giving

This gift is the special ability to contribute materially, above tithes and offerings, to the building of the Kingdom. It is not the kind of giving, such as tithes and offerings, that is expected of all Christians. It is the ability to give joyfully and generously to supply material needs.
The Greek word, *metadidoomi*, means "sharing of material possessions."[29]

The motivation of the Giver is to:
- Give to the physical needs of the body
- Contribute to others in order to support them in the extension of the Kingdom
- Entrust their own personal assets to others for the furtherance of the ministry

The need met in the body: MATERIAL

Characteristics (Strengths)
- Generously gives money, possessions, time, and self to others by the leading of the Holy Spirit
- Sees God as their provider and source
- Prefers to give anonymously, without recognition
- Handles own finances and resources well

Potential Pitfalls (Weaknesses)
- May give away resources that are needed by the family
- Want to control the gift – wanting it to be used their way
- Can use giving to avoid other spiritual responsibilities

Examples of the Givers in Scripture:
The widow who gave two mites (Mark 12:41-44), Abraham (Genesis 13, 14, 22, 23, 24)

Favorite scripture of the Giver: Proverbs 31:20
She extends her hand to the poor,
Yes, she reaches out her hands to the needy (NKJV).

Administrator/Leader

This gift is the special ability God gives which enables the person to see the goals of a group or organization and provide effective plans to accomplish those goals.

The Greek word, *proistemi*, literally means "to stand before" hence, "to lead, attend to" (indicating care and diligence), and is translated "to rule"[30] in Romans 12:8. It is also translated "maintain" in some instances (1 Timothy 3:8, 14).

The motivation of the Administrator is to:
- Direct, or provide leadership, in the accomplishment of goals for the smooth and orderly operation of the church
- Coordinate the activities of others for the achievement of common goals
- Care for the functional tasks, organize people and resources to accomplish the goals and vision

The need met in the body: EFFECTIVENESS, LEADERSHIP

Characteristics (Strengths)
- Highly motivated, organized, enthusiastic, efficient, and productive
- Focuses on the accomplishment of goals and gets the job done
- Take-charge type of person, has strong convictions, decisive, persuasive
- Able to see down the road, can visualize the resources and people necessary to accomplish the goal

Potential Pitfalls (Weaknesses)
- Can be too focused on goals and become insensitive to the needs of the workers
- "Workaholic" tendency – self-driven to the neglect of personal/family needs
- Micromanaging delegated tasks

Examples of Administrators in Scripture: The Proverbs Woman (Proverbs 31:10-31), Nehemiah

Favorite scripture of the Administrator: 1 Corinthians 14:40
  Let all things be done decently and in order. (NKJV)

Mercy/Compassion

This gift is the special ability God gives "to feel genuine empathy and compassion for individuals, both Christian and non-Christian, who suffer distressing physical, mental or emotional problems, and to translate that compassion into cheerfully doing deeds that reflect Christ's love and alleviate suffering."[31]

The Greek word, *eleeo*, means "to feel sympathy with the misery of another," and especially sympathy manifested in actions, or "to have pity or mercy on, to show mercy."[32]

The motivation of the person gifted with Mercy is to:
• Identify with and bring comfort and relief to those who are hurting or in distress.

The need met in the body: EMOTIONAL

Characteristics (Strengths)
• Deep-feeling people, are ruled by the heart rather than the head
• Tender-hearted, focuses on the emotional and mental needs of those who are hurting
• Very accepting, looks for the good in others
• Rejoices in the blessings of others, grieves the pain of others

Potential Pitfalls (Weaknesses)
• Easily hurt by other's comments or attitudes
• Tendency to take up other people's offenses
• May rush in to relieve suffering and in so doing, hinder God's work in the person (human compassion vs. godly compassion)

Examples in Scripture of those gifted in Mercy: Esther, The Good Samaritan (Luke 10:29-37)

Favorite scripture of the Mercy person: Romans 12:15
Rejoice with those who rejoice [sharing others' joy], and weep with those who weep [sharing others' grief] (AMP).

As we grow and mature, we may operate in any of the gifts at specific times. We may not all have the gift of exhortation, but we can certainly encourage one another. We may not all have the gift of serving, but we can all serve the body. We may not all have the gift of giving, but we should all give into the Kingdom. However, when you discover your gifts, you can begin to develop and exercise them for His glory.

Next is a very brief overview of the other two categories of gifts listed in the Word. As previously mentioned, for further teaching on these gifts, see the resources listed at the end of this book.

MINISTRY OR OFFICE GIFTS

Ephesians 4:7-16

These gifts are referred to as the gifts of the Son because verse 8 states: [Jesus] *led captivity captive, And gave gifts to men.*

The word "gift" in Ephesians 4:8 is the Greek word *doma* and it means "a present or a gift."[33] This word specifically refers to the Ministry, or Office Gifts, and refers to a person who is an equipper of the body of Christ. In other words, the "gift" is the person. These specially endowed human "gifts" to the body of Christ are those whom God has called to lead and serve in the office of apostle, prophet, evangelist, pastor, and teacher. These leaders have the responsibility of equipping the saints (Ephesians 4:12) and are important in seeing that the other two categories of gifts, listed in Romans 12:6-8 and 1 Corinthians 12:4-10, are applied in the body of Christ.

EQUIPPING means "making fit, preparing, training, perfecting, making fully qualified for service."[34] It has the sense in the original language of setting a bone during surgery.

So, equipping implies a recovered wholeness as when a broken limb is set and mends. The Great Physician is about adjusting His body so it will not be "out of joint." Part of the equipping work of the Ministry Gifts is to help believers identify their personal gifting and understand how that fits with others, so that *the whole body is joined and knit together by what every joint supplies, according to the effective working by which every part does its share, causes growth of the body for the edifying of itself in love* (Ephesians 4:16).

The Ministry Gifts are also referred to as the Five-Fold Ministry Gifts.

They are equipping ministries and are meant to work together, as a team, for the ultimate purpose of the church, as stated in Ephesians 4:13:

...till we all come to the unity of the faith and of the knowledge of the Son of God, to a perfect man, to the measure of the stature of the fullness of Christ.

While any believer may, at times, be used to teach, prophesy, lead people to the Lord, or "pastor" others in the sense of caring for them, it does not mean he or she is called to the office of teacher, prophet, etc. Those who are called to serve in the capacity of a Ministry Gift have been commissioned by God and been given spiritual authority for leadership that is more far-reaching in scope than the authority every believer has in Christ. Their gift is recognized and confirmed by leadership in the church. Jesus is the perfect example of the Five-Fold Ministry Gifts. He is the Apostle, the Prophet, the Evangelist, the Pastor/Shepherd, and the Teacher.

MANIFESTATION GIFTS OR GIFTS OF THE HOLY SPIRIT

1 Corinthians 12:4-11, 1 Corinthians 14: – Word of Wisdom, Word of Knowledge, Gift of Faith, Gifts of Healings, Working of Miracles, Prophecy, Discerning of Spirits, Gift of Tongues and Interpretation of Tongues.

These gifts are referred to as the gifts of the Holy Spirit because in 1 Corinthians 12:7 it states:

*But the **manifestation** of the Spirit [emphasis added] is given to each one for the profit of all.*

The word translated "manifestation" is the Greek word *phanerosis* and is from a root word meaning "to make apparent"[35] or make evident. It also means "exhibition or bestowment."[36] So the gifts listed in this passage give visible evidence of the activity of the Holy Spirit.

The classical, Pentecostal teaching explains that these gifts are not heightened natural abilities, or enhancements of natural talent, they are supernatural abilities, endowments, or gifts, bestowed on a person by the Holy Spirit. They are distributed to each person as the Spirit wills (1 Corinthians 12:11).

The Holy Spirit bestows the gifts to whom He wills as the occasion recommends from the divine viewpoint.[37]

In other words, as the Spirit sees the need in the particular situation or setting, He gives the appropriate gift to the person who is open to receive and exercise the gift so that everyone benefits (for the profit of all).

Harold Horton, one of England's Pentecostal pioneers, expresses God's purpose in giving these spiritual gifts:

God has designed in these heavenly endowments instruments for the revelation of His will, for the building up of His church, for the inspiration of His worshippers, for the amelioration (betterment) of the distressed, for the frustration of the plans of the adversary, and for the irresistible furtherance of the glorious affairs of the glorious kingdom of His ever-glorious Son.[38]

The chapters in 1 Corinthians that deal with the gifts of the Holy Spirit are bookends to chapter 13: Paul's teaching on love. Love for God and His Body must be the motivating force behind using the gifts and abilities He has given us. Without His love for us, we have nothing to give. Without His love in us, whatever we give would be empty...like sounding brass or a clanging cymbal (1 Corinthians 13:1).

Conclusion

As you discover gifting "threads" that your Heavenly Father has woven into your being, you will realize that you may have more than one gift that is predominant in your life. You are a unique combination of gifts, personalities, and abilities, lovingly knit and woven together into a wonderful package called YOU! (Psalm 139) You and I may have the same gift, but we will express it differently.

When each of us is functioning in our gifting, the tapestry of our individual lives becomes more apparent and the design God has imprinted upon us comes into greater focus. We see our lives from His perspective – a beautiful tapestry– a work of art – created by the Master Weaver.

Knowing your true identity in God is not an end in and of itself. It will help you to grow in your relationship with God and bring healing to the places of brokenness in your life. Your relationships with others will become stronger and healthier as you embrace and enjoy who God made you to be. The importance of knowing your identity is in being able to take the place God designed for you as part of HIS SELF-PORTRAIT, so that His image can be expressed in the earth and His kingdom may be advanced.

Let's Talk About It

1. Which of the Motivational Gifts do you most identify with? Share an example of how the gift(s) are expressed in in your life.
2. In what ways will knowing your gifting help you to understand and accept others who are gifted differently?
3. What Potential Pitfalls of your gift do you feel prone to? Share ways that you can overcome them and strengthen your gift at the same time.

At Home This Week

Using a concordance, look up the word "gift" or "gifts" in the New Testament. Make note of the different Greek words and their meaning. Ask the Holy Spirit to bring understanding and revelation to your heart concerning His gifts in you.

Truth to Embrace

1. All of these gifts, while diverse, are given by one Spirit. They come from the greatest gift – the Holy Spirit – and are visible evidence of His presence and activity in a believer's life.
2. Part of the equipping work of the Ministry Gifts is to help believers identify their personal gifting and understand how that fits with others, so that the body is ...*joined and knit together by what every joint supplies, according to the effective working by which every part does its share, causes growth of the body for the edifying of itself in love* (Ephesians 4:16).
3. When each of us is functioning in our gifting, the tapestry of our individual lives becomes more apparent, and the design God has imprinted upon us comes into greater focus. We see our lives from His perspective – a beautiful tapestry – a work of art – created by the Master Weaver.

DIVINE IMPRINT

Remember the mirrors I mentioned in Chapter Three? In this chapter, we want to look into the mirror of God's Word to discover our true identity in God. Let's go back to our text in Isaiah 62. You remember that in speaking to Jerusalem, God said He would give her a new name, no longer Forsaken and Desolate.

Isaiah 62:4b-5
But you shall be called Hephzibah, and your land Beulah;
For the LORD delights in you, And your land shall be married.
For as a young man marries a virgin,
So shall your sons marry you;
And as the bridegroom rejoices over the bride,
So shall your God rejoice over you.

Hephzibah and Beulah. Interesting names with great significance.

Hephzibah means "my delight is in her."[39] It is derived from a root word meaning something valuable, desirable.[40] It's a name that expresses love and security and speaks of favor. The word, "delight," (*chafets* in Hebrew) means very attractive, to be favorably disposed towards, to cherish, to be bent or inclined toward, to take pleasure in. Those words describe how God feels about us.

Beulah is a name that means married.[41] Married to the Lord! He likens His joy and delight in Jerusalem to that of the bridegroom rejoicing over his bride. Marriage had the connotation of protection for the woman, a place of safety. It also spoke of fruitfulness.

New Name, New Identity

In changing Jerusalem's name from Forsaken and Desolate to Hephzibah and Beulah, the Lord is also giving her a new identity. No longer will she live under names of reproach and shame; rather, the Lord is bestowing upon her names of honor and favor. He is calling her out of the captivity of the past that was filled with rejection and barrenness, into an understanding of who she truly is: His bride, cherished, protected, and fruitful.

And so the Lord speaks to us!

I believe He is saying to us, individually and corporately, just as He said to His Son, *You are My beloved, on **YOU** My favor rests* [emphasis added] (Luke 3:22 The Jerusalem Bible). He is bringing us out of the brokenness, rejection, and pain of the past, unraveling and undoing the tangled, discolored, and broken threads the enemy has woven into our lives. He is bringing us into a good land where we are more than enough to bring forth what is on His heart.

Deuteronomy 8:7-9

*For the LORD your God is bringing you into a good land, a land of brooks of water, of fountains and springs, that flow out of valleys and hills; a land of wheat and barley, of vines and fig trees and pomegranates, a land of olive oil and honey; a land in which you will eat bread without scarcity, in which **you will lack nothing**...;* [emphasis added]

In the context of this study, the "good land" is knowing that our value is based on three things:

- We are created by God, in His image.
- We are chosen by God.
- We are beloved of God.

Created by God, In His Image

We know that we are all made in God's image (Genesis 1:26), but did you know that He had a plan in mind for you before He ever said, "Let there be light" (Ephesians 1:4)?

He had a hand in fashioning you, forming you, while you were still in your mother's womb (Psalm 119:73; 33:15). He was involved in your life before you ever were! Henri Nouwen puts it this way:

From all eternity, long before you were born and became a part of history, you existed in God's heart. Long before your parents admired you, or your friends acknowledged your gifts, or your teachers, colleagues and employers encouraged you, you were already" chosen." The eyes of love had seen you as precious, as of infinite beauty, as of eternal value.[42]

His Tapestry

I mentioned in Chapter One that we are each a part of the tapestry of His self-portrait, and that He is also creating a unique tapestry in our individual lives. Ephesians 2:10 tells us that
We are His workmanship, created in Christ Jesus for good works...

"Workmanship" is the Greek word *poem,* and it means "a product, i.e. fabric"[43] and refers to that which is made by God. We truly are His tapestry!

Nowhere in Scripture do we see so clearly the intimacy with which God is involved in our creation as in Psalm 139:13-16.

If you are familiar with this passage, allow the Holy Spirit to bring fresh revelation to your heart.

Psalm 139:13
For You formed my inward parts; You covered me in my mother's womb.

God created you and formed you while you were in your mother's womb. The word "covered" is better translated "interwoven." In the physical sense, it speaks of the white bones, red arteries, blue veins all woven together, like a tapestry!

The same thought is repeated in verse 15:
My frame was not hidden from You,
When I was made in secret,
And skillfully wrought in the lowest parts of the earth.

"Frame" refers to the bones, and "wrought" means embroidered with many colors. Earth is a metaphor for the womb. This means you were "woven" by God – physically, spiritually, emotionally, with all the gifts and talents He designed just for you while you were yet in your mother's womb.

Psalm 139:16
Your eyes saw my substance, being yet unformed.
And in Your book they all were written,
The days fashioned for me,
When as yet there were none of them.

"Substance...unformed" is language that pictures clay that has not yet been formed into a pot, or a skein of thread that is not yet unrolled or woven.[44] Have you ever seen a needlepoint picture before any of the stitches have been sewn? There is a pattern, or design, stamped on a piece fabric. You follow the pattern as you begin to stitch with needle and thread. That's the picture of "unformed substance."

God had a design for you before your first day and has been weaving a tapestry of your life ever since. In His book, He wrote down all the days of your life, all the events you would experience, all the pain and all the joy that would make up your life, before you had lived even one day. Even though some of the stitches were not of His making, He saw... He knew...and He loved. He knows you intimately and He loves you immensely.

Fearfully and Wonderfully Made

Psalm 139:14
I will praise You, for I am fearfully and wonderfully made;
Marvelous are Your works,
And that my soul knows very well.

You are fearfully and wonderfully made! "Fearfully" doesn't mean afraid; rather, it means with respect or awe.[45] God took great care in creating you. You were not without forethought. You were not an afterthought. Your presence here on earth was not an accident. There are no accidents in God.

I mentioned my grandson Zach earlier. He is a child some might call an "accident" because he was born out of wedlock. My daughter wrote something so touching and profound in his baby book while he was still in her womb. To her yet-unborn son she wrote: "Some would say you were an unplanned pregnancy. That is not true. You just weren't planned by me."

This precious little boy is now a grown man. There's not space enough to share with you the untold joy and love he has brought to my daughter and our entire family. You see, he was planned by his heavenly Father and he is here by design.

Wonderfully means "to distinguish, to put a difference between, recognizable, to show marvelous."[46] God made you distinct, unique from any other person in the world. Brothers and sisters, even twins, are not exactly alike. God gives each of us special DNA that makes us different from anyone else. In natural terms, we think of ourselves as being a composite of two—mother and father. In reality, we are a combination of three—mother, father, and heavenly Father. A part of your heavenly Father is woven into your very being. He put His "designer signature" on you. You're not a Versace original, or a Calvin Klein or an L.A. Gear; you are a G.A.O.–God Almighty Original!

The Word Heals

This verse (Psalm 139:14) brought revelation and healing to my own life many years ago. I shared in Chapter Five that my father was absent while I was growing up, even though he was physically in the home until I was twelve. The Lord revealed to me that, while it took both my mother and father to bring me into the world, I only identified with my mother due to the lack of relationship with my father. Because of that, it was as if a part of my identity was missing, hence, the image of myself with no face. Faceless. Unrecognizable.

Why the face? I realized the face instantly distinguishes one person from another. When I read that I was "wonderfully made," it was the voice of my Father telling me: "You are recognizable, distinguishable, special. You have always been recognizable to Me. The feeling you had as a child was wrong. You have always been special to Me!" What healing that brought to my heart.

About the same time, I read an illustration that touched my heart: "In heaven, God carries around a picture of us in His hand and shows it to everyone. 'Look!' He cries out, 'This is my daughter. Isn't she wonderful?' He gently touches the picture as He speaks. 'I can hardly wait to see her face-to-face!'"[47]

The Bible says it this way: *Behold, I have indelibly imprinted (tattooed) a picture of you on the palm of each of My hands* (Isaiah 49:16, AMP).

God loves you so much, He not only had a hand in your creation, He has your picture imprinted on His hands!

Chosen by God

Paul said: *...he chose us in Him before the foundation of the world* (Ephesians 1:4).

The Amplified Bible says it this way:
Even as [in His love] He chose us [actually picked us out for Himself as His own] in Christ before the foundation of the world, that we should be holy (consecrated and set apart for Him) and blameless in His sight, even above reproach, before Him in love.

For He foreordained us (destined us, planned in love for us) to be adopted (revealed) as His own children through Jesus Christ, in accordance with the purpose of His will [because it pleased Him and was His kind intent]...

Jesus said: *You did not choose me, but I chose you and appointed you that you should go and bear fruit* (John 15:16).

Peter, quoting the OT said: *You are a chosen generation, a royal priesthood, a holy nation, His own special people* (1 Peter 2:9).

We are chosen. The problem is, when we hear "chosen," we think of being picked for a team, like when we were young. Chosen implies good…not chosen implies bad. It means some are left out. What if I'm the one left out?

But it's not that way with God! In God's economy, to be chosen doesn't mean others are rejected. There is no competition or comparison in being chosen. Chosenness is a decision made from His compassionate and loving heart. God's capacity is such that chosenness with Him is all inclusive – no one is left out.

The word "chosen" is an interesting Greek word. It is the word *eklegomai*. It means "to lay forth in a systematic way."[48] I think of Lego toys…laying out blocks in a systematic way to build something!

Before God ever said "Let there be light," He chose you, and began to systematically lay forth His design, His plan, and His purpose for your life! That gives your life immense value and worth!

Beloved of God

God chose us, and made us, and He also loves us greatly. An assembly line worker "makes" a product in the factory, but it doesn't mean he loves what he made. But God does. God's very nature is love (1 John 4: 7-8). His love for us is not founded in who we are but in who HE is. That is why our behavior is not the criterion for receiving His love.

Jesus admonished His disciples to love their enemies as well as their neighbors, so as to be like their Father in heaven (Matthew 5:43-48). He says that God sends the sun to rise on the evil and on the good, and sends rain to the just and unjust.

Just as it is the nature of the sun to shine, both on evil and good, so it is God's nature to shine His love on us. He loved us long before we ever knew Him (1 John 4:9-10). While we were still sinners, He sent His Son to die for us that we might know His love (Romans 5:8). The high cost the Father paid to make us His own – the Blood of His Son – gives us a value that cannot compare to anything the world has to offer. He so loved the world that He gave.

Oh that our hearts would comprehend the magnitude of that love!

Brennan Manning says it powerfully:

Living in the awareness of our belovedness is the axis around which the Christian life revolves. Being the beloved is our identity, the core of our existence.

In solitary silence we listen with great attentiveness to the voice that calls us the beloved. God speaks to the deepest strata of our souls, into our self-hatred and shame, our narcissism, and takes us through the night into the daylight of His truth: "Do not be afraid, for I have redeemed you; I have called you by your name, you are mine. You are precious in my eyes, because you are honored and I love you...the mountains may depart, the hills be shaken, but my love for you will never leave you and my covenant of peace with you will never be shaken" (Isaiah 43:1, 4; 54:10).

Let us pause here. It is God who has called us by name.

The God beside whose beauty the Grand Canyon is only a shadow, has called us beloved.

The God beside whose power the nuclear bomb is nothing, has tender feelings for us....

Define yourself radically as one beloved by God. This is the true self. Every other identity is illusion.[49]

Ephesians 3:20 says, *Now to Him who is able to do exceedingly abundantly above all that we ask or think, according to the power that works in us.*

It's a verse we often quote when petitioning the Lord in prayer. But have you ever considered the context in which this verse appears? In the Amplified Bible, Ephesians 3:17-19, reads:

May Christ through your faith [actually] dwell – settle down, abide, make His permanent home – in your hearts! May you be rooted deep in love and founded securely on love,

That you may have the power and be strong to apprehend and grasp with all the saints (God's devoted people, the experience of that love) what is the breadth and length and height and depth [of it];

[That you may really come] to know – practically, through experience for yourselves – the love of Christ, which far surpasses mere knowledge (without experience); that you may be filled (through all your being) unto all the fullness of God – [that is] may have the richest measure of the divine Presence, and become a body wholly filled and flooded with God Himself!

This entire passage is speaking of knowing the love of God. When we come to verse 20, it is a cry that God would do over and above what we could ask or think in revealing His love to us!

That is the prayer of my heart, that God would divinely reveal to you, the immensity of His love and the incredible value and identity you have in Him!

The Song of Solomon is a beautiful book that gives us a glimpse of the Bridegroom's heart for His Bride. One verse in particular reveals the effect that we, His beloved, have on Him.

Song of Solomon 4:9:
You have ravished my heart,
My sister, my spouse;
You have ravished my heart
With one look of your eyes,
With one link of your necklace.

The word "ravished" is the key. This Hebrew word has several meanings, the most significant of which is "to beat faster."[50] This means that when we just lift our eyes to Him in love, glance at Him, His heart beats faster! In other words, one look from us makes His heart skip a beat! It is awesome to realize that Jesus loves us that much.

Our Incredible Value

The story is told of a man who loved gems. He went to a gem show one day and walked up and down the aisles perusing all the stones available for sale. Some were very costly. Others went for pennies.

He stopped at one booth and picked up a rather large, blue-violet stone. Compared with the others on display, it was not particularly pretty. He looked at the stone, then at the price: $15.

He said to the owner: "You want $15 for this stone?"

"Well," replied the owner, "It isn't as pretty as the others, so I'll give it to you for $10."

The man took his wallet from his back pocket, hands trembling, and gave the merchant a $10 bill. As he walked away, he couldn't believe his good fortune. You see, the unattractive gem was a 1,905-carat natural star sapphire, appraised at 2.28 million dollars!

It took the lover of gems to recognize the value of the stone. Just as it takes the Lover of our souls to recognize our true value. To the world around us, we may not seem attractive or valuable, but in God's economy, our worth is "far above rubies" (Proverbs 31:10), or sapphires, or diamonds.

Despite our flaws and weaknesses, He loves us still (Psalm 103:11-14).

The Bigger Picture

The result of knowing that we are specially created by God, chosen by Him before the foundation of the world, and that we are His beloved, enables us to view ourselves differently – as altogether lovable and immensely worthwhile. Something happens when we see ourselves in that light: we begin to see the chosenness and belovedness in others. We are more accepting of their weaknesses because we've embraced our own. Jesus said that the world would know us by our love. The best way to love others is to first see our own belovedness.

Let's Talk About It

1. The name "Hephzibah" means, His delight is in you, and "Beulah" means, married. Since your marriage to Jesus Christ (salvation), how have you felt His delight? His protection? Safety? Provision?
2. Psalm 139 uses the word "fearful" – with respect or awe. God is saying you are awesome! Share the ways you see the awesomeness of who you are as a G.A.O. Discuss ways your relationships have become stronger and healthier as you have become more secure in your identity.

At Home This Week

1. Paraphrase Psalm 139 putting it in your own words. As you meditate on this Psalm, insert your name in the verses to personalize it.
2. Meditate on the following verses to understand further who you are in Christ.

2 Corinthians 5:17, 1 Corinthians 6:19, 1 Peter 1:18-19,
Galatians 3:13, 1 Corinthians 1:2,
Romans 8:17, Ephesians 1:13, Ephesians 1:6, Colossians 2:10,
Romans 8:1, Ephesians 2:19,
Matthew 5:13-14, 2 Corintians 5:21, 1 Peter 2:24, 2 Peter 1:4,
Ephesians 1:4,
1 Peter 2:9, Ephesians 2:10, Deuteronomy 32:10, Psalm 17:8,
Colossians 3:3, John 15:3, 9, 14-16.

Truth to Embrace

1. He is saying to us, individually and corporately, just as He said to His Son, *You are My beloved, on you My favor rests* (Luke 3:22).
2. God had a design for you before your first day and has been weaving a tapestry of your life ever since.
3. The high cost the Father paid to make us His own – the Blood of His Son – gives us a value that cannot compare to anything the world has to offer.

THE BRIDE
The Portrait Completed

As I have studied Isaiah 62:1-5 and asked the Lord about the significance of His changing Jerusalem's name in relation to her identity, I felt impressed that there was something in that for us, as His people: It is a picture of the progressive unfolding of us as His Bride. It is a season where He is bringing us out of the captivity of the past with the distorted identity the enemy and the world have given us, into an understanding of our true identity in Him as His Bride.

A natural body can be diseased in ways that prevent it from functioning in a healthy manner. Some physical disorders cause a disconnect between the brain and other parts of the body, such as limbs or organs. Results can range from involuntary movement like tremors, to atrophy of body tissue or organs. The latter condition is a wasting away or failure to grow in a normal manner, rendering the body dysfunctional.

That can be an apt picture of the Body of Christ. Different parts function according to their own understanding, following their own agenda, without proper connection to the Head. They are focused on their ministry, their calling, their anointing. The outcome is a lack of unity. Dysfunction. Lack of strength. Failure to grow in a strong, healthy way.

But a bride…that's a different story! She is joined to her beloved, her focus is solely on him. She is one with him.

Think with me for a moment about a bride before the wedding day. First, there is a time of preparation. Months before the wedding, there are many details to attend to: selecting a church, reception hall, guest list, invitations, flowers, cake, etc. During this busy time, the bride is more or less self-focused. It can be a time of great stress and tension. Having seen four daughters married, I am well acquainted with all the preparations that go into the wedding day!

I believe God has had us, His Bride, in a time of preparation, weaving us, if you will, into the tapestry of His self-portrait.

Wilderness

Preparation can feel like a wilderness. Before God does a new thing, there is usually a wilderness experience (Isaiah 43:18-19). As the tapestry takes shape, there are scissor snips and needle pokes that don't feel very good. We have been going through a cleansing and purifying as He deals with the issues of our hearts. That tends to cause us to be focused on ourselves.

Many have experienced breakings, emptying, fire, and other testings as God has been readying His Bride. In recent years we have seen God purifying His people by exposing sin and allowing trials that are intended to bring us forth as gold.

In his book, Pray for the Peace of Jerusalem, Tom Hess states,
Our degree of readiness for the wedding feast of the Lamb is often determined by our response to the trials we experience.[51]

Deeper Intimacy

Hosea 2:14:
Therefore, behold, I will allure her,
Will bring her into the wilderness,
And speak comfort to her.

He has allured us into the wilderness. In this reference, the wilderness is not a place of punishment, but a place of privacy, intimacy. He wants to speak to her heart. The Hebrew word, *leb*, meaning heart, is translated "comfort." Used here as an adverb, it means to speak tenderly, comfortably.[52] It is used similarly in Isaiah 40:2:

Speak comfort to Jerusalem, and cry out to her,
That her warfare is ended,
That her iniquity is pardoned.

He has been drawing us by His Spirit to pursue a deeper intimacy with Him. It is in that place of intimacy, in the secret place of the wilderness, that our identity is forged, personally and corporately.

John the Baptist came from years of wilderness living knowing who He was and who He wasn't. When the priests and Levites asked him if he was the Christ (John 1:19-23), he didn't use the opportunity to promote his own ministry or in any way lift himself up. Rather he clearly stated that he was NOT the Christ, he was merely the voice of one crying in the wilderness. He was merely the one who prepared the way for the Messiah.

It was John, when his disciples came to him concerned that he was losing followers to Jesus' ministry, who said, *He must increase, but I must decrease* (John 3:22-30). John was very clear about his identity. He never performed a miracle, he never healed the sick, yet Jesus said...*among those born of women, there has not arisen one greater than John the Baptist* (Matthew 11:11).

Paul was separated as an apostle from his mother's womb, yet in adult life became a persecutor of the church. After his Damascus Road conversion (Acts 9:1-19), rather than going to Jerusalem to confer with the other apostles, he went into Arabia for three years (Galatians 1:11-18). The Bible gives no account of those years, but it was probably a time of transformation for Paul – from persecutor to apostle – to prepare him for the mighty work God had for him.

Jesus was led by the Spirit into the wilderness (Luke 4:1). But after the wilderness...power!

Then Jesus returned in the power of the Spirit to Galilee, and news of Him went out through all the surrounding region (Luke 4:14-15).

As I shared about my own identity journey in previous chapters, it was in the secret place that God began to deal with my heart and unravel the identity I tried to weave with such things as performance and people pleasing. But most importantly, it was in the place of intimate relationship with Him that He began to show me how valuable I was simply because I was His, and that He had a wonderful plan for my life.

In the wilderness, we learn dependency. We come to know Him in a way we didn't know Him before, and we find we can trust Him completely (Song 8:5).

Hope from Trouble

Hosea 2 continues:
I will give her her vineyards from there,
And the Valley of Achor as a door of hope;
She shall sing there,
As in the days of her youth,
As in the day when she came up from the land of Egypt.
"And it shall be, in that day,
Says the LORD, That you will call Me 'My Husband,'
And no longer call Me 'My Master,'"

He will give her vineyards…from the place of intimacy will come fruitfulness, just as a bride brings forth children from the intimacy with her husband.

The Valley of Achor would be a door of hope. Achor means "trouble" and it was the place where Achan sinned by taking the plunder prohibited by God (Joshua 7). Verse 15 is a profound declaration: Hope would spring forth from the place where trouble or trial once was. In the midst of God's preparation of His Bride, there is hope for the future wedding feast of the Lamb. We have the hope that, as the church comes into the unity of spirit as His Bride, God will use us corporately, to bring in the imminent harvest of souls.

Verse 15 also speaks of her coming up from the land of Egypt. What was the identity of the Israelites in Egypt? They were slaves. They were in bondage. They built the physical structures of Egypt by the sweat of their brows and the fear of man.

God wants to bring us, His people, out of the captivity of the past – out of the identity distorted by the devil and the world system. He wants us to build His structure, His kingdom, not by flesh but by His Spirit. Not as slaves, but as His Bride: *You will call Me 'My Husband,' and no longer call Me 'My Master.'* It is not by striving in our own strength that we become His Bride. Rather, it will be as we hear Him speak of His love for us that we respond, and are transformed into His Bride.

Leaving the Identity of the Past

It can be difficult to break free from the identity of the past when the beliefs we hold about ourselves are so strong. The generation of Israelites that came out of Egypt was not the same one that took possession of the land. They could not get past the slave mentality and perished in the wilderness. Joshua and Caleb were the only two from that generation to enter the Promised Land. They knew who they were in God and that He kept his promises.

I once read about the way elephants are trained. It's amazing that a 10-ton fully-grown elephant can be held with the same size stake in the ground that holds a baby elephant weighing 300 pounds. Why? When they are babies, they are chained to the stake and they tug and tug, trying to pull themselves free. It may take hundreds of tugs before they realize they can't get away from that stake. Eventually, they stop trying. Their "elephant memory" takes over and they remember for the rest of their lives that they cannot break free from the stake. So, although it would take just one flick of the grown elephant's foot to be free, they remain chained to the stake in the ground.

We can be like that. Chained to the identity of the past, we are staked to the places where we've been told, "You're not enough.... you don't measure up...you'll never succeed." But a way has been made for us to be free!

The Blood of Jesus releases us from the stakes of the past, from the distorted and misshapen identity that has held us captive. When we know and experience the Truth, His power sets us free – free to embrace our true identity. We have a choice. We can decide to tug at that stake one more time, believing once and for all, what God says about us. We can choose the truth over the lie. When once we make that choice, God comes to us in His love and His power and leads us into the identity He had in mind for us all along.

No More Baals

Hosea 2:17 continues:
For I will take from her mouth the names of the Baals,
And they shall be remembered by their name no more.

The names of the Baals represented false gods or idols. An idol is anything that takes the place of God in our hearts. So, all the places we look to for identity – people, positions, possessions, ministry – can become idols in our lives. We think that in them we will find value, security, love, significance...life. But God is changing that in His people in this hour. He has been highlighting the truth about identity because He is shifting our focus from ourselves to our Bridegroom. He is giving us eyes only for Him.

The Father is radically committed to giving His Son a bride worthy of the King. He is not coming back for a bride who yawns in His face on Sunday morning, or who has other affections. He's coming back for a bride who wants Him as much as He wants her![53]

At the Altar

Back to the bride... we've said there was a time of preparation, and now the wedding day finally arrives. She is getting ready for the big moment! Making sure her dress is just right, her veil is set, every hair in place, make-up just so, she is still, to some degree, focused on herself. But, as she steps to the back of the church and lifts her eyes to the altar, there stands her beloved. She forgets about her gown, her veil, everything...she has eyes only for him! So it is with us. As we behold our Bridegroom, our focus shifts from us to Him.

A recent movie called The Runaway Bride offers some interesting insights. The underlying theme is a young woman in her search of her identity. The movie is about a young woman who has been to the altar three times, only to panic and run at the last minute, leaving the groom abandoned and alone.

Toward the end of the film, she has once more fallen in love and is ready for the special day. Just before the wedding, Ex-fiancé #3 offers some advice to the prospective bridegroom: "You've got to maintain eye contact," he says, pointing to both eyes. "Eye contact! If you lose eye contact with her, she'll break and run."

The bride begins to walk down the aisle. Her groom waits expectantly at the altar, eyes riveted on his lovely bride. Halfway to the altar, she hesitates, her step falters, you catch your breath thinking she's about to run again. But she smiles, regains her composure, and continues toward her beloved, nearly reaching the front of the church.

Suddenly, someone snaps a photo and the flash momentarily blinds the groom, causing him to close his eyes and blink. Eye contact is broken! A look of panic sweeps over her face as she turns on her heels and runs out of the church. (You'll have to watch the video to see how it ends!)

I couldn't help thinking about the Bride of Christ as I watched. We are facing challenging times. If we don't maintain eye contact with our Bridegroom, we'll likely break and run, too. Our intimate, face-to-face relationship with Jesus is that which will sustain us as we follow Him and come to know Him and love Him more deeply.

A marriage is not made on the wedding day… that is only the beginning. A marriage is built day-by-day through a heart commitment one to another and is strengthened by both wilderness experiences and mountain-top encounters. In a similar way, a tapestry is created painstakingly stitch-by-stitch, thread-by-thread, unraveling and raveling, until the image is fully formed. We take comfort in knowing our Bridegroom is committed to perfecting His Bride and seeing to it that there are no spots or wrinkles in our wedding gown (Ephesians 5:26-27).

Releasing His Favor

I believe we are in a season when, as Isaiah 62:5 says, our Bridegroom is rejoicing over us, His Bride, and is releasing new favor upon us. Again, thinking about the natural bride on her wedding day, what happens when the strains of the Wedding March begin to play, and the bride proceeds down the center aisle? The entire congregation rises and turns to face her as she walks by.

That is a picture of what the Scripture says will happen when Jerusalem's true identity is seen: *Gentiles shall see her righteousness and kings her glory* (Isaiah 62:2).

Isaiah 62:12:
> *And they shall call them The Holy People,*
> *The Redeemed of the LORD;*
> *And you shall be called Sought Out,*
> *A City Not Forsaken.*

These verses speak of favor being released upon the church, His Bride, so that the eyes of the world are turned toward the church, just as the eyes of the congregation turn toward the bride. God wants to showcase His bride to the world. However, it doesn't always come in the way we think!

Tragedy to Testimony

Remember Columbine? The events of April 20, 1999 that unfolded at Columbine High School in Littleton, Colorado, USA, were hard to believe. Twelve students and one teacher were killed, and twenty-four other students were injured in the shootings. The tragedy shocked the nation. Yet, the subsequent Christian witness that came out of that tragedy was broadcast throughout the media in the United States and around the world. One young student, Rachel Scott, died acknowledging Jesus Christ as her Lord. The eyes of the world being turned toward the church.

In the aftermath of the horrific events of September 11, 2001, we learned of ordinary men, strengthened by their faith, who became heroes, sacrificing their lives to save others. Todd Beamer, 32, recited Psalm 23 just before he and three other passengers overcame the hijackers of Flight 93. Tom Burnett, 38, told his wife via cell phone to "Pray, just pray." Once again, amid tragedy and heartache, the testimony of Christians has been heard and read around the world. The eyes of the world being turned toward the Church.

Habakkuk 1:5
> *Look among the nations and watch— Be utterly astounded!*
> *For I will work a work in your days*
> *Which you would not believe, though it were told you.*

Destiny of the Bride – The Portrait Completed

God is doing an awesome work in this hour among His people. He is bringing us out of a past of woundedness, slavery, and shame, into an identity and destiny as His Bride:

A Bride who is BEAUTIFUL!
A Bride who is CONFIDENT!
A Bride who is SECURE!
A Bride who is VICTORIOUS!
A Bride who is FRUITFUL!

As we come into the understanding of our incredible value and destiny in Christ, we will no longer minister out of a place of need, but from a heart that has been healed and restored. No longer desiring to satisfy the emptiness inside through the things we do, we can give to others from a heart motive that is pure. The more we realize how much God loves us, the more our focus turns outward to touch others with His love.

In Genesis 48:20, Jacob blessed his grandsons with powerful words that became a blessing throughout Israel:

So he blessed them that day saying, By you Israel will bless, saying, 'My God make you as Ephraim and Manasseh!'

The name Ephraim means, "For God has made me forget all my toil (grief, pain, anguish) and all my father's house" – in other words, the pain of the past.

Manasseh means, "For God has caused me to be fruitful in the land of my affliction."

This blessing was a declaration that one's negative past would be forgotten and their future would be fruitful. Just as a young bride is fruitful in bringing forth new life, so His Bride is destined to bring forth life through His purposes in the earth.

He is not interested in a church's self-centered existence. He is not looking for it to survive or merely to grow. He is looking for the Church to fill the earth with His glory, to subdue the earth and have dominion over it, to triumph over the principalities and powers, to be ready as the Bride of Christ. God is getting His Church worldwide ready for a final push towards the final mighty harvest.[54]

As He brings us out of the captivity of the past identity into our new identity in Him, we will take our place alongside one another as His Bride. Fulfilled in Him, the striving will diminish (Philippians 3:3), the jockeying for position will cease (Joel 2:7-8), and we will move ahead as one to accomplish together, what we cannot do alone (Ecclesiastes 4:9-12).

Synergy

Synergy is a phenomenon that occurs when two or more parts working together create a greater influence than the sum of each of the parts. Let me give you an example. At a livestock show, the winning team of horses in a Horse Pull event pulled 5,000 pounds. The runner-up team pulled 4,000 pounds. You would expect that together they would pull 9,000 pounds. However, together they pulled 13,000 pounds. That's synergy. A biblical example is Leviticus 26:8:

Five of you shall chase a hundred, and a hundred of you shall put ten thousand to flight…

Think of the synergistic power released as the Bride works together to see the Bridegroom accomplish what is on His heart for the Kingdom!

Unity is the place where God commands the blessing (Psalm 133:3). The goal of being healed of the identity of the past is greater than our personal identity. It enables us to be satisfied with the stitch and color of the thread that we bring to the tapestry of God's portrait. The greater purpose of knowing our personal identity is coming together as one, so His image can be brought forth in the earth as the completed self-portrait He desires…the finished tapestry, the Bride.

Psalm 45:10-15
Listen, O daughter, Consider and incline your ear;
Forget your own people also, and your father's house;
So the King will greatly desire your beauty;
Because He is your Lord, worship Him.
And the daughter of Tyre will come with a gift;
The rich among the people will seek your favor.
The royal daughter is all glorious within the palace;
Her clothing is (inter)woven with gold.
She shall be brought to the King
in robes of many colors (embroidered garments);
The virgins, her companions who follow her, shall be brought to You.
With gladness and rejoicing they shall be brought;
They shall enter the King's palace.

Let's Talk About It

1. Describe a time in your life that you would define as a wilderness experience. Did it bring you into deeper intimacy with the Lord? Share how.
2. In what ways do you see yourself as a Bride approaching her wedding day? What preparations have you made?
3. Do you remember a time when you "broke eye contact" and became a Runaway Bride?
4. Share ways in which you feel:
   BEAUTIFUL in Christ.
   CONFIDENT in Christ
   SECURE in Christ
   VICTORIOUS in Christ
   FRUITFUL in Christ

At Home This Week

Meditate on Isaiah 54, particularly the promises to the Bride:
You will expand to the right and to the left
Your descendants will inherit the nations
They will make the desolate cities inhabited.
You will not be ashamed
You will not be disgraced, nor put to shame.
You will forget the shame of your youth,
You will not remember the reproach of your widowhood – bereavement,
forsaken, discarded (like a divorced person).
Your Maker is your husband
Your Redeemer is the Holy One of Israel, the God of the whole earth.
I will gather you with great mercies
I will have mercy on you with everlasting kindness.
I swear – I will not be angry with you, nor rebuke you.
Though the mountains depart, and the hills be removed,
My kindness will not depart from you
My covenant of PEACE will not be removed.

Peace is used 250 times in Old Testament and is not just absence of strife. The word, "peace" (shalom) encompasses all of the following elements:

Completeness	Safety	Perfectness – maturity
Wholeness	Soundness	Fullness
Health	Tranquility	Rest
Welfare	Prosperity	Harmony
Contentment		
Absence of agitation or discord		

More than the absence of war and conflict, it is the wholeness for which the entire human race seeks. That is His promise to His Bride! That is our identity and destiny as His Bride!

Receive these promises into your heart as you begin to walk in your true identity in Christ!

Truth to Embrace

1. I believe God has had us, His Bride, in a time of preparation, weaving us, if you will, into the tapestry of His self-portrait.
2. He has been drawing us by His Spirit to pursue a deeper intimacy with Him. It is in that place of intimacy, in the secret place of the wilderness, that our identity is forged, personally and corporately.
3. The greater purpose of knowing our personal identity is coming together as one, so His image can be brought forth in the earth as the completed self-portrait He desires...the finished tapestry, the Bride.

EPILOGUE

Perhaps as you look over your life, it seems all you see is the underside of the tapestry with its knots, missed stitches, frayed ends, and threads that seem to go nowhere. Maybe you feel your tapestry is far from a work of art.

I want to assure you, although you see only the underside right now, your Bridegroom's vantage point from above allows Him to see the completed tapestry, and it is altogether lovely in His sight.

We are all in process. For some the process has just begun. It can be uncomfortable, even painful, when God begins to unravel and snip away the threads the enemy has sewn into our lives.

There must be a commitment to stay with the process until God has completed the work and you begin to see the beautiful pattern and purpose of your life emerge. God had a "finished product" in mind when He created you – He sees you in the fullness of the identity He intended when He knit you together in your mother's womb. He is committed to finishing what He started:

Philippians 1:6
Being confident of this very thing, that He who has begun a good work in you will complete it until the day of Jesus Christ;

That means that even in those times when you want to "break and run," He is right there, running alongside you, calling you back to Himself so He can pour His unconditional love upon you day by day.

Psalm 138:7-8
Though I walk in the midst of trouble, You will revive me;
You will stretch out Your hand
Against the wrath of my enemies,
And Your right hand will save me.
The LORD will perfect that which concerns me;
Your mercy, O LORD, endures forever;
Do not forsake the works of Your hands.

These verses speak to us as we are in the midst of the process. As we yield to the work of His Spirit in our lives, difficult though it may be,

He will revive us. He will *perfect that which concerns me*: that is, He will continue to work out His purposes in us until we come into the fullness of who He created us to be. He wraps His loving purposes around all the sins, failures, and hurts of our lives and changes them. His grace is the enabling power of the Holy Spirit to transform us from the distorted identity of the past, to our true identity as His Bride.

THE PLAN OF THE MASTER WEAVER

Our lives are but fine weavings
That God and we prepare,
Each life becomes a fabric planned
And fashioned in His care.
We may not always see just how
The weavings intertwine,
But we must trust the Master's hand
And follow His design.
For He can view the pattern
Upon the upper side,
While we must look from underneath
And trust in Him to guide.
Sometimes a strand of sorrow
 Is added to His plan,
And though it's difficult for us,
 We still must understand,
That it's He who fills the shuttle,
It's He who knows what's best,
So we must weave in patience
And leave to Him the rest.
Not till the loom is silent
And the shuttles cease to fly,
Shall God unroll the canvas
And explain the reason why –
The dark threads are as needed
In the Weaver's skillful hand
As the threads of gold and silver
In the pattern He has planned.

Author Unknown

In closing...

My prayer is that through this book, you have been encouraged to see and appreciate the wonderful and unique tapestry that God is weaving of your life…your true identity! You truly are a work of art! I pray, too, that you've caught a glimpse of the awesome self-portrait God is creating as each of us embraces our part in His design. May the eyes of the world see His Bride as never before!

ABOUT THE AUTHOR

Diane M. Fink

The heart of Diane Fink's ministry is to see transformed lives, transformed cultures, and transformed nations. Desiring to bring Spirit-empowered change to others through her speaking, writing, and prophetic ministry, she imparts practical wisdom, spiritual insights, and sound Biblical teaching. In addition to *Faceless*, Diane has authored several studies, numerous articles, and teaching materials, many on relationship and God's heart for His people.

Her heart for the Middle East and Muslim nations was birthed through a prophetic word and empowered by a supernatural encounter. *Asmara Transformed* is a booklet Diane authored geared toward reaching Muslim women. It is a story of friendship between an English teacher and a Muslim woman.

Ordained as minister and commissioned as prophet by her church, she equips people throughout the United States and has spoken in more than 20 nations in Europe, the Middle East, and Asia. As part of the prophetic team at her church, she participates in prophetic ministry oversight, speaks at conferences, and has developed a School of the Prophets for Seattle Bible College. She enjoys teaching, imparting, and encouraging others in their gifts.

Having served in leadership for more than 30 years in an international, trans-denominational ministry, she has a broad perspective of the Body of Christ and God's movement among His people.

Diane serves on the Board of Directors of Marked, a ministry among orphans in Mexico, dedicated to empowering them to radically transform their lives and change their culture. She also serves as an Advisor for Sought Out, a ministry whose goal is to impact lives through personal encounters with the Holy Spirit in real and tangible ways.

She lives in Everett, Washington, and has four grown daughters and several grandchildren.

Resources for further study:

Jane Hansen Hoyt, *The Journey of a Woman*, Regal Books, 1998.

Loren Cunningham, *Why Not Women?* YWAM publishing, 2000.

Robert S. McGee, *The Search for Significance*, Word Publishing, 1985, 1990.

Henri Nouwen, *Life of the Beloved*, Crossroad Publishing Company, 1993.

Henri Nouwen, *Here and Now, Living in the Spirit*, The Crossroad Publishing Company, 1994.

(Actually, anything written by Henri Nouwen)

Brennan Manning, *Abba's Child*, NavPress, 1994.

Craig Hill, *The Ancient Paths*, Family Foundations Publishing, 1992.

Don & Katie Fortune, *Discover Your God-Given Gifts*, Chosen Books, 1987, 2002.

C. Peter Wagner, *Your Spiritual Gifts Can Help Your Church Grow*, Regal Publishing, 2005.

Harold Horton, *The Gifts of the Spirit*, Assemblies of God Publishing House, 1934.

Larry Randolph, *User Friendly Prophecy*, Cherith Publications, 1995.

Larry Randolph, *Spirit Talk*, MorningStar Publications, 2005.

T. Austin Sparks, *Prophetic Ministry*, Destiny Image, 2000.

ENDNOTES

Chapter 2
1. Max Lucado, The Applause of Heaven, (Word Publishing, 1990), pgs. 170-171.
2. Spirit Filled Life Bible, (Thomas Nelson Publishers, 1991).
3. Vine's Expository Dictionary of Biblical Words, (Thomas Nelson Publishers, 1985), pg.298.
4. The Online Bible Thayer's Greek Lexicon and Brown Driver & Briggs Hebrew Lexicon, (Woodside Bible Fellowship, Ontario, Canada, 1993). Licensed from the Institute for Creation Research.
5. Biblesoft's New Exhaustive Strong's Numbers and Concordance with Expanded Greek-Hebrew Dictionary, (Biblesoft and International Bible Translators, Inc, 1994).

Chapter 4
6. Adam Clarke's Commentary, Electronic Database, (Biblesoft, 1996).

Chapter 5
7. George Barna, The Barna Update. Retrieved 5.21.07 from barna. org: http://www.barna.org
8. Ibid.
9. Marie Powers, Shame, Thief of Intimacy, (Gospel Light, 1998), pg. 26.

Chapter 6
10. Ibid., Biblesoft Strong's
11. Loren Cunningham, Why Not Women? (YWAM publishing, 2000), pg. 18.Ibid., Biblesoft Strong's
12. Ibid. pg. 19.
13. Rick Joyner, The Morning Star Prophetic Bulletin, July 1999, pg. 7.
14. Gary Smalley, John Trent, The Blessing, (Thomas Nelson Publishers, 1986).

Chapter 7
15. Mike Bickle, adapted from The Pleasures of Loving God, (Creation House, 2000).
16. Robert S. McGee, The Search for Significance, (Word Publishing, 1985, 1990), pg. 41.
17. H. Norman Wright, A Dad Shaped Hole in My Heart, (Bethany House Pub-lishers, 2005).
18. Life Recovery Bible, (Tyndale House Publishers, 1992) pg. 665.
19. Webster's New World Dictionary, (Simon and Schuster,1982).
20. Julia Cameron, Vein of Gold, (Tarcher/Putnam, 1996), pg.3.

Chapter 8
21. Henri Nouwen, Here and Now, Living in the Spirit, (The Crossroad Publishing Company, 1994), pg. 61-62.

Chapter 9
22. Ibid., Biblesoft Strong's
23. Ibid.
24. Ibid.
25. Ibid.
26. Ibid., Vine's
27. C. Peter Wagner, Your Spiritual Gifts Can Help Your Church Grow, (Regal Publishing, 2005), pg. 33.
28. Ibid., Biblesoft Strong's
29. Ibid., Thayer's
30. Ibid., Vine's
31. Ibid., Wagner
32. Ibid., Vine's
33. Ibid., Biblesoft Strong's
34. Ibid.
35. Ibid.
36. Ibid.
37. Ibid., Spirit Filled Life Bible
38. Harold Horton, The Gifts of the Spirit, (Assemblies of God Publishing House, 1934), pg. 38

Chapter 10
39. Ibid., Biblesoft Strong's
40. Ibid.
41. Ibid.
42. Henri Nouwen, Life of the Beloved, (Crossroad Publishing Company, 1993), pg. 45.
43. Ibid., Biblesoft Strong's

44. Ibid., Spirit Filled Life Bible
45. Ibid., Thayer's
46. Ibid., Biblesoft Strong's
47. Heather Harpham, Daddy Where Were You?, (Aglow Publications, 1991), pg. 78.
48. Ibid., Biblesoft Strong's
49. Brennan Manning, Abba's Child, (NavPress, 1994), pg. 57-59.
50. Ibid., Thayer's

Chapter 11
51. Tom Hess, Pray for the Peace of Jerusalem, (Progressive Vision International, 2000).
52. Ibid., Vine's
53. Bob Sorge, message at an Aglow International Conference, November 1999.
54. Brian Mills, Time for Change, Friday Fax 2000, issue 45, November 10.